Asked and Answered:
Your Guide to Law School Success

Volume 2

Advice for Second-Year Law Students

By

Donna Gerson
Contributing Editor,
Student Lawyer magazine
(American Bar Association)

THOMSON

™

WEST

Mat #40754598

© 2008 Thomson/West
  610 Opperman Drive
  St. Paul, MN 55123
  1–800–313–9378

Printed in the United States of America

ISBN: 978–0–314–19485–5

TEXT IS PRINTED ON 10% POST CONSUMER RECYCLED PAPER

Table of Contents

Section 2:

Introduction

Asked and Answered addresses the issues that matter most to law students: practical questions and answers pertaining to academic and career success, featuring tips from the experts. The inspiration for the *Asked and Answered* series arose from the desire to offer law students straightforward answers to their most commonly asked questions.

The *Asked and Answered* series provides useful answers from the experts—successful lawyers, law firm recruiting managers, law school professors, administrators, and career services professionals. The collective wisdom of these professionals will enable you to make informed choices about your career path.

The phrase, "asked and answered," derives from the Rules of Evidence and stipulates that a question must be disallowed in court if it has already been asked by the interrogator and answered by the witness. In plain English, it translates into "been there, done that."

As a lawyer and former career services director, I meet with hundreds of law students every year when I lecture about the legal profession. Whether I visit a top-tier or bottom-tier law school, most of the questions I am asked remain the same: Will I find a job this summer? What types of jobs are available if my grades are average? What steps can I take to achieve peak academic performance in my second year? What can I do to distinguish my résumé from the others? How can I best prepare for an interview? What interview questions will I be asked? Who should I contact to learn more about a particular practice area?

Asked and Answered will help you get the facts quickly, with easy-to-read lists, tips, and first-hand advice from the experts. The questions and answers in this book follow a second-year law student through the course of an academic year, from preparing for the on-campus interviewing process to tips for a successful, fulfilling summer.

If you have additional career-related questions after reading this volume of *Asked and Answered,* then e-mail them to me at donna@donnagerson.com. Life can be mysterious; law school should not be. If you have questions, let me help you find the answers.

–Donna Gerson

Section 1:
On-Campus Interviewing

The first semester of your second year is synonymous with three words: "on-campus interviewing" or OCI, the process for finding a summer job following your second year. This section will discuss the ins and outs of OCI, what to expect in terms of timing, credentialing, and the process of securing a summer jobs through your law school's OCI program. In addition, this section will address job fairs, specialty interview days, and other job-search issues.

Let's begin with some preliminary questions regarding summer employment, hiring criteria, and your responsibilities as a job candidate.

Q. Must I find a law-related job for the summer following my second year, or can I just relax after a really stressful school year?

A. "Yes, you absolutely need to find a law-related job this summer!" says Carla J. De-Velder, director of the Notre Dame Law School Career Services Office. Here's why, according to DeVelder:

· If you have your eyes on a medium to large law firm for your post-graduate employer, you need to be in their summer associate program during your second summer. Most of these employers hire from their summer classes and opportunities for third-year candidates with no prior relationship with the firm are limited. Smaller firms need associates who can hit the ground running and who bring, at least, one summer's worth of real-life skills.

· If you have your heart set on a government agency or public interest organization, you should be working in such a position during your second summer. These employers also tend to hire students they know and who have worked for them in the past. They, too, need new lawyers with real life experience. On top of that, they want to see in you a deep interest in and commitment to the type of work they are doing. It will be awfully hard to convince a prosecutor's office during an interview held your third year that you desire, above all else, a career in criminal prosecution if there is absolutely nothing on your résumé that reflects this commitment! At best, the employer will think you are uninformed and possibly misguided. At worst, they will think you are disingenuous or coming to them as a second or third choice. Either way, you won't get the job.

Why is working in a legal venue so important this summer? DeVelder explains it this way: "Law school teaches you very little about the actual practice of law. Employers want to see that you have experienced a bit of the 'real world' and that you have a modest skill set that will help decrease your learning curve. Look at it this way: all things being equal, if you had one candidate who had no experience on their résumé and another who had two summers of solid work experience that related to the job for which they are interviewing, who would you choose? Experience equals marketability, even at this early stage of your career."

Whether you work for a large, mid-size, or small firm, government agency, public interest organization, as a faculty research assistant, or with a judge, the practical skills you acquire will be transferable to your next employer and enable you to gain valuable experience and forge professional connections.

While most second-year students want and expect paid employment, remember that experience is the most sought-after goal here. For instance, if your dream job in international law is to work in The Hague this summer, then by all means pursue the dream, but understand the consequences. You may not be paid, but there are other important perks, such as specific experience, name recognition, and the opportunity to make professional connections.

Bottom line: You must find a legal job for the summer following your second year!

Q. What credentials will impress a legal employer?

A. Legal experience always impresses employers. Why? Lawyers want to understand that you are motivated to practice law, have taken the steps to gain some experience, and have some substantive skills upon which to build. Lawyers are always interested in candidates who can "hit the ground running" and have a modicum of confidence about both their abilities and their career path. No one wants to hire someone who appears unsure about their career choice, who lacks basic experience, and who needs an enormous level of hand-holding.

Do not worry if you have not had a glamour job at a large national firm, the Supreme Court, or the United Nations. Focus, instead, on learning the fundamentals and building a résumé that demonstrates your commitment to practice law and provide substantive skills such as:

- Conducting legal research
- Drafting documents
- Writing briefs, motions or memoranda
- Attending depositions, trials, or arbitration panels

These types of work experiences carry weight with most legal employers and enable them to determine if you have the right set of skills to be helpful in the office.

Q. What criteria should I seek in a potential summer employer?

A. Before delving into the details regarding OCI, pause for a moment and consider what criteria you ought to be looking for in a summer employer. There is no "one-size-fits-all" work experience. You must find the right match for your individual interests, skills, credentials, and career aspirations.

For your second summer job, the stakes are a bit higher than your first summer. For your first summer, the advice you received was: do anything in a legal venue, try something different, and build your résumé with substantive experience that puts your academic studies to practical use.

For your second summer, the focus ought to be on beginning to narrow your practice area interests and also—if possible—trying to lay the groundwork for where you may want to end up after graduation. After all, in some—but not all—cases a second summer job may come with a full-time offer at the conclusion of the summer. While that is the case generally with large firm summer associate programs, there are also some federal and state agency summer programs, as well as some small and mid-size firms, that extend offers of employment following second summer. Therefore, where you work for the summer may have an impact on your long-term career plans. This isn't always the case, but at the very least, your second summer job is yet another in a line of employment opportunities that will help you build your case for the next job search.

With that in mind, look for a summer employer with three qualities in mind:

1. Location
2. Practice area
3. Fit

In terms of location, second summer is your opportunity to narrow down where you may want to work following graduation. Not only will this help you build a convincing résumé, but also it will help you make connections in that market. Furthermore, narrowing down where you want to settle eventually will inform your decision about where you take the bar exam, an issue that's looming on the horizon.

While you do not have to commit to a particular practice area at this juncture, it can be helpful for you to begin narrowing the scope of choices. This will enable you to research more effectively, draft a more compelling cover letter, and focus your job search. No one can do a fifty-state job search in all practice areas. Those types of mass mailings are time-consuming, expensive, and unsuccessful. However, if you can identify a city or two that interests you and couple that with some parameters around ideal practice areas, then you can focus your job search more efficiently.

The final quality is the hard-to-describe concept of fit. Do you like the people at the law firm? Do you "click" with those around you? Do you see yourself practicing there and developing a book of business? In general, do you enjoy your day-to-day work at the firm? These are the questions that you can ask yourself to determine if there's a good "fit" with the firm.

Criteria to Guide Your Job Search

- Location
- Practice Area
- Fit

Q. What are my responsibilities as a job candidate?

A. As a job candidate, you must be honest, behave in a professional manner, own responsibility for your job search, and adhere to all of the timelines set forth by employers and your career services office.

The National Association for Law Placement (NALP) created Principles and Standards to guide law students, law schools, and legal employers in the job search process. Part 3 pertains to law students who are candidates for jobs, and states:

A. Candidates should prepare thoroughly for the employment search process.

1. Before beginning an employment search, candidates should engage in thorough self-examination. Work skills, vocational aptitudes and interests, lifestyle and geographic preferences, academic performance, career expectations and life experiences should be carefully evaluated so that informed choices can be made. General instruction should be obtained on employment search skills, particularly those relating to the interview process.

2. Prior to making employment inquiries, candidates should learn as much as possible about target employers and the nature of their positions. Candidates should only interview only with employ-

ers in whom they have a genuine interest.

3.   Candidates should comply with the policies and procedures of law schools whose services they use.

B. Throughout the employment search process candidates should represent their qualifications and interests fully and accurately.

1.   Candidates should be prepared to provide, at employers' request, copies of all academic transcripts. Under no circumstances should academic biographical data be falsified, misrepresented, or distorted either in writing or orally. Candidates who engage in such conduct may be subject to elimination from consideration for employment by the employer, suspension or other academic discipline by the law school, and disqualification from admission to practice by bar admission authorities.

2.   Candidates should be prepared to advise prospective employers of the nature and extent of their training in legal writing. Writing samples submitted as evidence of a candidate's legal skills should be wholly original work. Where the writing was done with others, the candidate's contribution should be clearly identified. Writing samples from law-related employment must

be masked adequately to preserve client confidentiality and used only with the permission of the supervising attorney.

C. Throughout the employment search process students should conduct themselves in a professional manner.

1. Candidates who participate in the on-campus interview process should adhere to all scheduling commitments. Cancellations should occur only for good cause and should be promptly communicated to the office of career services or the employer.

2. Invitations for in-office interviews should be acknowledged promptly and accepted only if the candidate has a genuine interest in the employer.

3. Candidates should reach an understanding with the employer regarding its reimbursement policies prior to the trip. Expenses for trips during which interviews with more than one employer occur should be prorated in accordance with those employers' reimbursement policies.

4. Candidates invited to interview at employer offices should request reimbursement for reasonable expenses that are directly related to the interview and incurred in good faith. Failure to observe this

policy, or falsification or misrepresentation of travel expenses, may result in non-reimbursement and elimination from consideration for employment or the revocation of offers by an employer.

D. Candidates should notify employers and their office of career services of their acceptance or rejection of employment offers by the earliest possible time, and no later than the time established by rule, custom, or agreement.

1. Candidates should expect offers to be confirmed in writing. Candidates should abide by the standards for student responses set out in Part V and should in any event notify the employer as soon as their decision is made, even if that decision is made in advance of the prevailing deadline date.

2. In fairness to both employers and peers, students should act in good faith to decline promptly offers for interviews and employment which are no longer being seriously considered. In order for law schools to comply with federal and institutional reporting requirements, students should notify the office of career services upon acceptance of an employment offer, whether or not the employment was obtained through the office.

3. Candidates seeking or preparing to accept fellowships, judicial

clerkships, or other limited term professional employment should apprise prospective employers of their intentions and obtain a clear understanding of their offer deferral policies.

E. Candidates should honor their employment commitments.

1. Candidates should, upon acceptance of an offer of employment, notify their office of career services and notify all employers who consider them to be active candidates that they have accepted a position.

2. If, because of extraordinary and unforeseen circumstances, it becomes necessary for a candidate to modify or be released from his or her acceptance, both the employer and the office of career services should be notified promptly.

F. Candidates should promptly report to the office of career services any misrepresentation, discrimination or other abuse by employers in the employment process.

G. Students who engage in law-related employment should adhere to the same standards of conduct as lawyers.

1. In matters arising out of law-related employment, students should be

guided by the standards for professional conduct which are applicable in the employer's state. When acting on behalf of employers in a recruitment capacity, students should be guided by the employer principles in Part IV.

2.   Students should exercise care to provide representative and fair information when advising peers about former employers.

A full list of NALP Principles and Standards can be found at www.nalp.org.

Your Responsibilities During the Job Search

- Behave in a professional manner
- Know the policies and procedures
- Respect deadlines
- Own responsibility for your job search
- Notify your career services office of acceptances, rejections, or any questionable behavior

---

What Is NALP?

The National Association for Law Placement, headquartered in Washington, D.C., publishes an annual Directory of Legal Employers, conducts salary and other career-related surveys, and serves as the bridge between law schools and legal employers on all matters related to hiring.

According to the NALP web site, "Virtually all ABA-accredited law schools and most of the largest legal employers of lawyers in the United States (large law firms, governmental agencies, and some corporations and public service organizations) belong to the National Association for Law Placement (NALP)." One of the fundamental reasons NALP was formed in 1971 was to promote fairness and informed decision-making during the recruitment process. Together, the law schools and employers belonging to NALP have developed and agreed to abide by the "NALP Principles and Standard," a set of guidelines that offers an ethical framework for all participants in the recruiting process.

"Under the NALP timing guidelines, employers are required to leave offers open for specified lengths of time to allow you to complete your interviewing schedule and make an informed decision about this important first step in your legal career. You also have certain ethical responsibilities affecting such areas as response dates and how many offers you can hold."

NALP's web site is www.nalp.org

Q. What is On-Campus Interviewing (OCI)?

A. On-campus interviewing (OCI) is the primary way that many large employers hire second-year law students for summer associate positions. While many students associate OCI with large national and regional law firms, many federal and state government agencies and public interest organizations also conduct their summer hiring process through OCI.

The OCI process will vary from law school to law school depending on many factors, such as how many employers visit your campus, the type of software program (if any) that your career services office maintains to administer OCI, the ranking of your law school, and the number of personnel in your career services office.

Because there is so much variation from school to school, the first piece of advice that I offer is simply this: When your law school offers "OCI Orientation" during the second semester of your first year, make sure you attend this program. Very important and specific information about application deadlines, procedures, and policies will be discussed during this orientation program. Miss this program and you will miss very important deadlines that may occur during the summer between your first and second years.

My second piece of advice is: Visit your career services office, preferably toward the end of your first year or during the summer between first and second year, to meet with a counselor. By the summer, you will have your first year grades and understand what options are available to you. A personal one-on-one meeting will also help you create a strategy that will help you succeed during your second summer job search.

The timing issues and procedures are extraordinarily important and you need to fully understand the schedule of deadlines and requirements to participate in OCI. Many students assume that OCI starts the first day of the fall semester; this is not the case. In some instances, OCI deadlines fall during the summer and employers begin interviewing on campus in August, before classes begin. You are responsible for meeting these deadlines; you, and nobody else but you.

In some instances, law firms will conduct interviews during July or August if you happen to be in town. For example, if you are attending law school in Atlanta but you want to work in Chicago and are spending your first summer in Chicago, it's not unusual for a Chicago law firm to conduct a screening interview in July or August when you're in town. It's convenient for everyone—you're in town, they're in town, everyone saves time and expense. So don't operate under the misconception that OCI begins on the first day of school. If you do, then you may be losing out on many good opportunities the summer prior to the start of your second year.

"The summer before your second year should be spent preparing for OCI," advises Laurel A. Hajek, Assistant Dean for

Career Services at The John Marshall Law School in Chicago. "It takes time to update your résumé, write a great cover letter, forge networking contacts, figure out the legal market, and keep track of all of the deadlines. Preparation takes time."

OCI To-Do List

- Attend your career services office "OCI Orientation" program, typically held at the end of your first year. Important deadlines, policies and procedures will be discussed at this meeting. Do not miss it!

- Schedule an appointment with your Career Services Office toward the end of your first year or during the summer between first and second year to discuss your personal plan for success.

Understand What OCI Is . . . and Isn't

OCI is a process that enables large employers (private firms, large federal and state agencies, and some very large public interest organizations) to hire in advance for the following summer. These jobs tend to be highly competitive, coveted positions with large employers (typically firms with 100 or more attorneys). Because these firms are very large, they are able to conduct hiring far in advance of the actual start date in order to secure their pool of talent for the summer from the largest array of candidates.

At large law firms, the position you are being hired for is called a "summer associate" position and this job comes with some very distinct perks. First, your salary for the summer is typically what a first-year associate earns on a pro-rated weekly basis. Take a look at the most recent salary numbers for first-year associates at the very largest law firms and—let's face it—it's a lot of money.

Second, you get to experience legal practice from the perspective of a very large law firm with all the pomp and circumstance that comes with the territory—posh offices, a secretary, meals at nice restaurants, and special summer associate events such as parties, picnics, and other entertainment.

The final perk of working as a summer associate is this: if you do well, and assuming you actually enjoy the work environment, then many large law firms are in the position to offer full-time employment to you, either at the conclusion of the summer or during the fall semester of your third year. In short, you're paid a great deal, learn the ropes, have fun being entertained, and can coast into your third year with a full-time offer in hand.

If OCI sounds too good to be true, well… it is. Depending on the ranking of your law school, only about 10% of your class can expect to find a job through OCI. At top-tier law schools, perhaps 50% will find jobs through OCI. In short, not everyone finds a job through OCI. Furthermore, even if you have the credentials and the desire to work at a very large firm, you may find that large law firm life is not a good match for you and you may be back to the drawing board during your third year. Even if you thought you had a great summer and think you're a good match for the firm, you still may not receive an offer of employment after your summer associate summer, thereby throwing you back into the employment pool looking for a full-time job during your third year.

Who Qualifies for OCI?

Any second-year law student in good standing is qualified to participate in OCI.

Who really qualifies for OCI?

Here's the 800-pound gorilla that's sitting next to you as you read this book: grades, class rank, and law school ranking are the three biggest factors that will influence whether or not you qualify to participate successfully in OCI. Let's discuss each in order:

- **Grades.** Most OCI employers will list a threshold GPA or class rank on their NALP Employer Form. Many employers will waffle with language such as "excellent academic credentials required" or words to that effect. The law firms want excellence, not mediocrity, in scholastic performance. Can you blame them? Here's where it gets fuzzy: your idea of academic excellence may differ from their definition of excellence. While no law firm will go on record with a bright-line answer about what constitutes "excellent academic credentials," understand that if you're not at least in the top 20% of your class—and depending on your law school's ranking in U.S. News & World Report, if you're not in the top 10% of your class—you probably won't get lots of attention from OCI employers.

Tip: If your school offers a difficult-to-interpret grading system, one that is less-than-transparent to employers, you need to explain this to employers. This is particularly important for employers who do not typically recruit from your law school and may be confused by a grading system that consists of something other than letter grades and the traditional numeric GPA, for instance. Therefore, if you attend a school that offers a system that is not readily understandable without an explanatory note, take action and explain yourself to employers so they can place you in the context of your class.

If you have questions, speak to your career services office for advice. You don't want to proceed on your own and then find out you've violated a law school policy about grade reporting.

- **Class rank.** Like grades, your class rank—where you stand relative to your classmates—will impact your success during OCI.

- **Law school ranking.** Where is your law school ranked relative to other law schools in your area and the U.S.? While law school deans and professors will argue that *U.S. News & World Report* rankings are flawed, the fact is that most law firms pay attention to the ranking of your school (in *U.S. News, The Gourman Report,* or elsewhere) and its reputation among members of the profession. The higher your law school's reputation, the deeper into a class a recruiting coordinator will search for a candidate. If you are attend a lower-tier school, understand that recruiting coordinators may be willing to look at the top five academic performers in your class.

This news about law school ranking can be very distressing for law students to hear, particularly during the OCI season. You chose a law school for various reasons and class rank was one of the criteria you may or may not have paid attention to in your decision-making process. While everyone believes that they can overcome a low ranking through exceptional academic performance, it's rarely the case. For an in-depth discussion of alternatives to OCI, see page 45.

Q. How does OCI work?

A. Every law school has different procedures for OCI. Some schools use software programs, such as Symplicity, to administer the process. Other schools still run OCI by submitting paper résumés to employers.

Some schools utilize a bidding system whereby law students are limited in the number of employers to whom they can apply; other schools do not place limits on student applications. In short, you must know what your law school's system entails. This means you need to attend the OCI orientation that is offered in the spring of your first year. If you are reading this now as a second-year student and don't know your school's process, then make an appointment immediately with your career services office.

Time Is of the Essence!

You snooze, you lose during fall OCI. Don't make the mistake that some very smart second-year students will when confronting OCI. Some students will look at the circus of OCI activity and say, "I'm going to wait until the law review students find their jobs and then look." Or, "most of the employers coming on my campus are from the East Coast. Since I want to work on the West Coast, I'll just wait until OCI is over and then visit my career services office to start my job search." Stop right there! The prime time to be searching for a job—particularly with larger firms and large government agencies—is between August and

---

October of your second-year. While small and mid-size firms tend to hire later in the year, some small and mid-size firms will also hire in the fall. Why forego opportunities by not being prepared?

A career services director shared the following story: "A very bright second-year student wanted to work in Chicago for her second summer. She perused the list of OCI employers visiting the law school and saw that the majority hailed from New York or Washington, D.C. Since she did not want to work in either Washington, D.C or New York, she did not participate in OCI nor did she conduct an independent job search in Chicago. She simply assumed that Chicago firms hired differently. In early October she happened to walk into the career services office and explained her situation. 'I'll just wait until all this OCI hoopla is over and then I'll start applying to the Chicago firms,' she said. Imagine her horror when she learned the truth about the time line for jobs nationwide. After a panicked meeting with a career services professional and a fast start, the law student began calling and writing to large Chicago firms. Luckily, her timing was a little late but still in the acceptable range. She managed to get a summer associate offer in Chicago and a full-time offer."

Moral of the story: Sometimes even smart students can do dumb things if they don't understand the complexity and strategy behind OCI. Don't make the same mistake!

Generally speaking, here's how OCI works:

- Résumés and other application materials such as transcripts or cover letters (if requested by an employer) must be submitted by a particular deadline.

- Application materials are forwarded to employers.

- The employer, often the legal recruiting coordinator or other professional tasked with submitting credentials, reviews the résumés to determine who ought to be interviewed. At some firms this is done by a staff professional; at other firms a committee reviews all of the résumés. Either way, résumés are reviewed and a determination is made to extend an invitation to interview.

- Employers will then contact either the career services office and/or individual students to let them know that they would like to conduct a "first interview" or "screening interview." These interviews typically will take place on campus. The on-campus screening interviews are generally between 20 and 30 minutes in length. Depending on many factors (the law firm's hiring needs, the reputation of the law school, the general quality of the candidates at your school), employers will send one or more interviewers to visit your law school. For screening interview tips, see page 29.

- Interviewers will usually be asked to rank the students they have interviewed that day. Depending on the law firm's hiring needs, interviewers will be instructed to recommend that a certain number of students be invited to visit the law firm for a call-back interview.

- Students will receive invitations to schedule call-back interviews either by phone, letter or e-mail. Call-back interviews are typically all-day experiences that take place at the law firm.

- A student should schedule a call-back interview as quickly as possible, since hiring decisions are made on a rolling basis at most firms. Therefore, earlier in the hiring season is better than later in the hiring season when fewer spots are available. For call-back interview tips, see page 32.

- After a call-back interview, an employer will take one of the following actions:

  • Make you a job offer on the spot (this is rare, but it happens);

  • Make you a job offer within a few days or weeks after the hiring committee meets and makes a decision;

- Hold an offer pending decisions from other law school candidates; or

- Send you a rejection letter.

For a discussion of accepting or rejecting offers, see page 34.

Screening Interview Tips

- **"You never get a second chance to make a first impression."** This adage is at the heart of the screening interview. Take these initial screening interviews seriously because the interviewers you are meeting are truly the gatekeepers to the next step in the OCI process.

- **Schedule a mock interview with your career services office.** Do not approach the interview process with a "let's see what works" approach. Instead, get coached about the typical questions you will be asked in a 20-minute screening interview and review what you ought to emphasize as well questions you ought to ask.

- **Dress appropriately.** Conservative interview suits are always winners. Look like the professional you want to become someday. Don't spend tons of money on clothing. One or two great interview suits and a few different shirts are all you need. One good pair of shoes will suffice.

- **Pay attention to grooming.** Get a haircut, pay attention to your nails, avoid cologne, and use mouthwash. These small details can mean a lot. Screening interviews often take place in tiny, windowless spaces. After a long day spent with many nervous law students, the rooms can become stifling, hot, and uncomfortable. You are in close quarters with interviewers, sometimes knee-to-knee at a small table. You may be the editor-in-chief of the law review, but you still need to pay attention to personal hygiene.

- **Come prepared with a question or two to ask.** Often an interviewer will ask, "do you have any questions for me?" The answer is always, "yes!" Asking questions indicates interest, enthusiasm and intellectual curiosity. Asking no questions means you're not interested and not engaged in the process. For a list of good questions to ask an employer, see page 165.

- **Write a thank-you letter immediately.** Even if decisions regarding call-back interview may be rendered almost immediately, proper etiquette requires that you acknowledge the interviewer with a short typed business letter of thanks. E-mail can also be appropriate. Not only will you demonstrate good manners, you tell the employer that you really care about the firm. You never know, it could tip the scales in your favor.

· A model thank-you letter can be drafted in advance on your computer and modified for each employer. It ought to be fairly straightforward and brief: "Thank you so much for the opportunity to interview with X, Y, Z firm. I thoroughly enjoyed our conversation today about the summer associate program. Based on our conversation, I would be honored to work at X, Y, Z firm this summer and contribute to the success of your firm. I look forward to hearing from you and thank you again for the chance to learn more about your work."

Tip: Keep track of your success rate with initial interviews. While there is no specific statistic for determining if you're doing well or not, keep this in mind: If you are participating in screening interviews with big firms and getting no call-back invitations (or very few), this is a sign that something is wrong! If you are frustrated with your progress, then you must contact your career services office for immediate advice and intervention. In some cases, students grossly misunderstand what they ought to be saying or doing during screening interviews. Some students may appear arrogant, inappropriate, or disinterested in the process and employers may have a negative impression. Whatever the issue may be, do not sit quietly and hope that things improve on their own. When you wait to get help, opportunities disappear. There is a short window of opportunity to interview during OCI (from August to mid-October). Take full advantage of this time span to do your very best.

Call-Back Interview Tips

· Be prompt about scheduling call-back interviews. Some law schools offer call-back days or a call-back week when classes are suspended in order for students to participate in call-back interviews. Try, whenever possible, not to miss class. However, scheduling call-back interviews ought to take place fairly quickly. Remember, offers are typically made on a rolling basis so scheduling early in the OCI season can be advantageous.

· Understand the rules for scheduling travel, hotel, and transportation and abide by the rules. Ask the firm legal recruiting coordinator if you are unsure. Typically, large law firms will pay for travel and hotel expenses. If you are interviewing with small or mid-size firms, inquire about reimbursement and don't be surprised if they do not offer this perk.

· If you are interviewing with more than one firm in a city, be sure to

---

tell the legal recruiting coordinator so that the firms can coordinate splitting your travel expenses. Not only do you consolidate travel, you deftly put firms on notice that you're a candidate who is in demand.

- Plan ahead if you're in an unfamiliar city. Anticipate rush hour traffic, know the exact location of the firm, and arrive 5 minutes early for your scheduled start time.

- All of the rules pertaining to screening interviews apply: dress appropriately, pay attention to grooming, and come prepared with a knowledge of the firm and questions to ask. For a list of questions you might want to ask, see page 165.

- For a longer discussion of interview tips, see page 29.

Tip: Take a lighter academic load during the first semester of your second year. It makes things manageable in terms of OCI. This semester is probably the most stressful and challenging. Make life a bit easier by taking one class fewer if possible.

Q. How many offers can I hold at one time?

A. Understand the rules regarding how many offers you may hold at one time and the various deadlines for dealing with holding several offers during the fall.

If you participate in OCI, then know the rules for timing of acceptances, holding offers, and rejections. The National Association for Law Placement (NALP), the organization that helps law school career services offices connect with legal employers to insure that the hiring process is fair, has established guidelines for law students and legal employer.

The following NALP Principles and Standards (Part V) are excerpts of interest to second-year students:

General Standards for the Timing of Offers and Decisions

To promote fair and ethical practices for the interviewing and decision-making process, NALP offers the following standards for the timing of offers and decisions:

A. General Provisions

1. All offers to law student candidates ("candidates") should remain open for at least two weeks after the date of the offer letter unless the offers are made pursuant to Paragraphs...C below, in which case the later response date should apply.

2. Candidates are expected to accept or release offers or request an extension by the applicable deadline. Offers that are not accepted by the offer deadline expire.

3. A student should not hold open more than five offers of employment at any one time. For each offer received that places a student over the offer limit, the student should, within one week of receipt of the excess offer, release an offer.

4. Employers offering part-time or temporary positions for the school term are exempted from the requirements of Paragraphs B...below.

5. Practices inconsistent with these guidelines should be reported to the student's career services office.

B. Summer Employment Provisions for Second and Third Year Students

Employers offering positions for the following summer to candidates not previously employed by them should leave those offers open for at least 45 days following the date of the offer letter or until December 30, whichever comes first. Offers made after December 15 for the following summer should remain open for at least two weeks after the date of the offer letter.

Students may request that an employer extend the deadline to accept the employer's offer until as late as April 1 if the student is actively pursuing positions with public interest or government organizations. Students may hold open only one offer in such circumstances. Employers are encouraged to grant such requests.

Employers offering positions for the following summer to candidates previously employed by them should leave those offers open until at least November 15.

Employers offering candidates positions for the following summer and having a total of 40 attorneys or fewer in all offices are exempted from the provisions of this section. Offers made on or before December 15 should remain open for a minimum of three weeks. Offers made after December 15 should remain open for at least two weeks.

For a complete text of NALP Principles and Standards, see www.nalp.org.

Q. I'm told that I'm "on hold" with a law firm. What does this mean? What should I do??

A. Being "on hold" is not a bad thing! Think of "on hold" status as being wait-listed at a college or law school. Law firms tend to hire on a rolling basis beginning as early as August of your second year. If a law firm has 50 summer associate slots available, then they will conduct screening and call-back interviews and make offers on a weekly, bi-weekly, or monthly basis. Earlier in the OCI season, there are more slots to fill and there is a strong incentive to make hiring decisions in order to fill the class. As the OCI season progresses and students accept offers, fewer slots remain available. As slots fill, firms may become a bit more conservative about candidates.

Generally speaking, the "slam dunk" candidates for whom there are no objections whatsoever will receive offers quickly. If you are a good candidate, but perhaps not a "slam dunk," then you might be put in a holding pattern as other candidates are considered.

Why are you "on hold"? There can be several reasons:

- Your interview was good but not great. You may have impressed some lawyers at the firm, but not others.

- Your credentials are good, but not great. Despite the fact that you received a call-back interview, there may be lingering concerns that your academic record is not strong enough or the firm desires candidates with some very specific credentials to fill a future hiring niche.

- Your law school may be new to this firm and the firm may hesitate to make a commitment.

- The legal job market is highly competitive and there are some really stellar candidates competing for very few slots.

Tips for Students in "On Hold" Limbo

- Being "on hold" is not a bad thing. It simply means that there are other candidates ahead of you in the queue, some may have better credentials or particular skills that interest the firm. You may still receive an offer (or you may not).

- Talk to your career services office and let them know you're "on hold." They can offer specific tips and insights into your situation.

- You must continue actively job-searching until you receive an offer from an employer.

- If you do receive an offer from another employer, notify the firm that has you "on hold." Sometimes a competing offer can be an incentive to a firm to make you an offer.

- Keep in contact with the law firm that has you "on hold" and stay on their radar. Don't harrass the firm or stalk the legal recruiting coordinator with daily or weekly contacts. Determine when the hiring committee meets (first and third Thursdays, for instance) and be sure to make a polite contact the business day prior so you maintain your presence.

- Stay positive. If you show frustration or impatience with a firm, it may only be held against you. If you receive an offer ultimately, you do not want to start your summer associate experience with whispers about your behavior leading up to your offer.

Bottom line: Don't take it personally. Take action. Some students may become paralyzed with being "on hold" at one firm, wait for a response, and do nothing in the interim. This is a very bad strategy. Keep a positive attitude and remember: Until you receive a job offer, you must continue searching actively for a job.

Q. I've been rejected by the law firm of my dreams! What should I do?

A. No one likes being rejected. It's an awful feeling, especially when your heart was set on a particular employer and career path that seemed perfectly right to you. Experiencing this type of disappointing rejection can be especially difficult in the high-stress, status-conscious environment of law school.

You've been rejected and an immediate opportunity is foreclosed at this time. Who knows what the future holds? A rejection from one firm today may turn into a subsequent offer as a lateral candidate a few years hence when you develop expertise in a particular practice area.

Tips to Deal with Rejection

- Acknowledge that you're upset and hurt. While it's deeply disappointing to be rejected, you have not received a bad diagnosis or something really horrible. The firm may have made a bad decision in your opinion, but that's the decision.

- Try to determine if the decision was based on something other than objective criteria such as grades or credentials. For instance, did you fare poorly in the interview process? Did you respond to a question with an inappropriate answer? Was your lunchtime etiquette appalling? Were you rude to support staff? Speak to your career services office about your situation. Sometimes discrete inquiries about your candidacy will reveal something that you can change in the future. For instance, you may inquire through career services and find out that you exhibited a knee-tapping tic that many people found odd and it overshadowed your great credentials.

- Avoid calling the firm yourself to inquire—delegate this to your career services office if possible. You may be too emotionally charged to have a conversation and there is the possibility that you will say something that you will regret later.

- Never denigrate the firm that rejected you. Lawyers tend to be well-connected and a bad word about Firm A will inevitably come to the attention of Firm A. Always put a positive spin on things. For instance, you can always say, "I was very disappointed not to receive an offer from Firm A. They were really great people and I would have been delighted to work there." Take the moral high road even if you are wounded at this time.

- Keep looking for a job until you receive a job offer. Some students deal with rejection by going into hibernation mode ("if no one wants to make me an offer, then I'm going to stop looking"). Avoidant behavior is not productive and you're only hurting yourself; you must continue searching for a job until you receive an offer.

· Write an acknowledgement letter to reiterate your interest. Sometimes a well-written acknowledgement letter may stand you in good stead next year. While you cannot depend on OCI during your third-year (it's very competitive with even fewer spots open than during second-year), you never know! You may have been an extremely close call at the firm and should a vacancy occur during third-year, you may be the next on the list. Always be a gentleman or lady in your dealings with firms, even in the midst of rejection upset.

Here is a sample acknowledgement letter that can be addressed either to the legal recruiting coordinator or hiring partner:

Dear Jane,

I was disappointed to learn that I did not receive an offer from X, Y, Z firm. I thoroughly enjoyed meeting everyone at the firm. X, Y, Z firm's practice areas align well with my professional interests and I would have been honored to contribute professionally to your firm's success. I wish you and everyone success in the coming year and hope that you will consider my credentials next year.

Sincerely,
John Student

Q. I see postings for specialty interview days that my school offers. What am I supposed to do with this information? Is this in conjunction with OCI?

A. In addition to OCI, many law schools offer specialty interview days in particular target cities such as Washington, D.C., New York City, Chicago, or other large metropolitan areas. These special interview days are either exclusive to your law school or in conjunction with other area law schools. For instance, the Philadelphia area law schools have traditionally offered a Four-in-One Interview Day for students in that city.

In many cases, law school alumni participate in these specialty interview days as interviewers. As a result, participating law firms or government agencies will be welcoming to your law school.

Find out if your law school offers specialty interview days in cities that interest you. These opportunities are designed in conjunction with OCI. This means that you need to stay abreast of application deadlines for these interview days and schedule time on your personal calendar to travel and be present for the interviews.

In short, specially designed interview days in other cities can be great opportunities to schedule several screening interviews in one day. Take advantage of these interview days, if possible. It is worth the time and travel expense in order to interview with a few employers in one city.

In addition to special interview days and job fairs that your school organizes and promotes, you can also participate in a number of specialty interview days that are offered to students based on practice area interests or minority status. See page 47 for a discussion of job fairs and interview days.

Q. I didn't receive an offer through OCI! Now what do I do?

A. Don't panic! You need to implement your personal Plan B. Every law student, regardless of one's class rank, ought to have a contingency plan in case your first choice of employer does not work out. Pinning all your hopes and dreams on OCI (or a job fair or a family connection) is a bit like walking into a casino with two quarters and hoping to hit the jackpot.

OCI is never a sure thing. Your grades may be excellent, but your interview style may be atrocious. You may be on the Law Review but your career aspirations lie in public interest law so large firm employers sensed your ambivalence to big firm life and took a pass on you. Your grades could have been great, your interview style impeccable, but you just hit some bad luck in a tough legal market and came up short.

"Plan B is the way most law students find jobs," says Laurel A. Hajek, Assistant Dean for Career Services at The John Marshall Law School in Chicago. "It's great if OCI works out but more likely than not it won't result in a job offer. Second-year law students need to look at other opportunities and determine their individual career goals. Ask yourself, 'what is it that you really want?'"

There's more to the legal profession than large firm practice and OCI. If your interests and credentials align with what large firms and government agencies focus upon during OCI, that's great. However, there are many options for students who either do not want the large firm experience or who may not have the necessary credentials. For instance, consider the merits of the following types of legal opportunities:

Small and Mid-size Firms

Only a small percentage of lawyers in private practice actually work at large firms. According to *The Lawyer Statistical Report: The U.S. Legal Profession in 2000* by Clara N. Carson (American Bar Foundation, 2004), only ten percent of all private practitioners in the U.S. work at firms of 100 or more attorneys. Most lawyers in private practice work in firms of 50 or fewer attorneys (the broadest definition of small firm) or in solo practice.

Most small and mid-size firms will not come on campus to conduct interviews. They are neither willing to hire so far in advance nor prepared to hire in the numbers that large firms typically do. So while your career services office will try its best to attract smaller firms, whether through fall OCI, spring OCI or special job fairs, it's highly unlikely that most small employers will make house calls to your law school. This means that the burden rests with you, the second-year law student, to research and seek out these employers.

"If you wanted to work for a big firm this summer but OCI did not pan out, consider applying to outstanding boutique firms in practice areas that interest you, explore in-house opportunities, or research the mid-size firm market" suggests Laurel A. Hajek, Assistant Dean for Career Services at The John Marshall Law School. "Spend your second summer building a specific set of skills that may interest big firms during OCI at the beginning of your third year."

For detailed information about small firm hiring practices, read my book *Choosing Small, Choosing Smart* (2nd ed., NALP, 2005). In addition, schedule time to talk to a staff professional in your career services office. Many law schools maintain very thorough lists of small firms in your city or region and can help advise you in your small firm job search process.

Federal and State Agencies

While some of the largest federal agencies, such as the Department of Justice and the Securities and Exchange Commission, participate in OCI, there are many smaller federal and state agencies that do not participate in OCI. Consult with your career services to determine the full range of federal and state agencies that hire and the timelines for hiring.

---

www.studentjobs.gov
Offers listings of federal government opportunities for students, along with links to other government sites.

Job Fairs

One of the best-kept secrets of the law school summer job search is the existence of so many job fairs across the country. Job fairs enable employers to gather in a centralized location and meet law students for the purposes of initial interviews.

Job fairs differ enormously in their scope and organization, so you need to conduct your research before your second year begins. Some job fairs require a pre-application process and screen candidates before inviting them. Other job fairs have strict requirements regarding eligibility. Still other job fairs invite applicants from particular law schools only. Below are the names of just a few of the job fairs offered throughout the U.S. Inquire at your career services office for more information and to determine deadlines and eligibility:

- American Intellectual Property Law Association (AIPLA) Job Fair
- Boston Lawyers Group Washington Area Job Fair for Students of Color
- Cook County Job Fair (Chicago)
- Delaware Minority Job Fair
- DuPont Legal Minority Job Fair
- Equal Justice Works (EJW) Public Interest Career Fair
- Florida Public Defenders Statewide Career Fair
- Hispanic National Bar Association Convention and Job Fair
- IMPACT Career Fair for Law Students and Attorneys with Disabilities
- Lavender Law Conference and Job Fair
- Loyola Patent Law Interview Program

- National Black Law Students Association Mid-Atlantic Job Fair
- Minnesota Minority Recruitment Conference
- Nashville Bar Association Minority Clerkship Program
- National Black Prosecutor's Association Annual Conference and Job Fair
- New Hampshire Job Fair
- Northeast Black Law Students Association Job Fair (NEBLSA)
- Northwest Minority Job Fair (Seattle, WA)
- BLSA Midwest Minority Recruitment Conference
- Council on Legal Education Opportunity (CLEO) Career Fair
- Heartland Diversity Legal Job Fair
- New Hampshire Legal Job Fair
- Philadelphia Area Minority Job Fair
- Rocky Mountain Diversity Legal Career Fair
- San Francisco Intellectual Property Law Association Bay Area Job Fair
- Southeast Minority Job Fair
- Southern California Interview Program
- Tri-State Diversity Recruiting Program (Kentucky, Indiana, and Ohio)
- Vault/MCCA Legal Diversity Job Fair
- Virginia Bar Association Diversity Job Fair

Tips to Implement Your Own "Plan B"

1. Get help earlier rather than later. Too many students delay coming forward with issues and waste valuable time during OCI, either because of procrastination, embarrassment, or a combination of the two. If you are getting lots of first interviews and very few call-back interviews, then assume that there's a problem and get to the career services office. Do not wait until Thanksgiving to ask, "I wonder what happened?" You may still be able to salvage some call-back interviews if you determine you're in trouble.

Often, the law students who say "I'm a great interviewer" tend to be the worst offenders. They don't realize how they are coming across, may be answering questions a bit too candidly, or demonstrate a lack of interest in the firm (even when they think they are showing interest in the firm). These types of shortcomings in interview style or content can be addressed, but only if you deal with them quickly.

Schedule a mock interview with your career services office. Ideally, you ought to schedule a mock interview before OCI begins so that you're in fighting form beginning with your very first interview. If you didn't think that far ahead or thought you would do better with interviews without coaching, then now is the time to meet with a career services professional and get help.

2. Acknowledge that OCI did not work out and determine why. If you went through

OCI and did not succeed in securing an offer, then it's a good idea to figure out why with the help of your career services office. While it's great to mull this over with friends or faculty mentors, the people to contact are your career services office. First, they can give you some clear, objective reasons based on your information. Second, they can discretely contact recruiting coordinators and get the inside scoop for you. This information can be very helpful to you as you move forward with Plan B.

3. Conduct research. Based on your personal interests, geographic desires, and academic standing, focus yourself and pinpoint your energies. Where do you want to work? What type of work interests you the most? If you can narrow down your area(s) of interest, it can help you focus on researching and finding those employers who may truly appreciate your credentials. You may be pleasantly surprised that your law school career services office maintains lists of small firms or can help direct you to other resources, job fairs, and mentors who are willing to advise you. Do not wait for a job posting to appear that fits your needs. Now is the time to be proactive, conduct the research, and network.

4. Remain positive in cover letters and interviews. If OCI did not work out and you are disappointed, tired, frustrated, and ready to give up, don't! And don't vent to a potential employer about how you really feel. Craft a story in your cover letter to future employers that highlights your credentials, gives a plausible reason for you to be applying for a particular job, and remains upbeat. In other words, be prepared to tell your story and put a potential employer at ease that you are, in fact, very interested in this particular job and that you would be a good "fit" with their practice. In order to create and tell a compelling story, be sure to rehearse with a mock interview through your career services office. A mock interview enables you to smooth out any of the rough spots in your narrative.

Spring OCI

While fall OCI offers the largest array of legal employers, many law schools offer smaller spring OCI programs. Employers who visit campus in the spring tend to be smaller law firms, some state or local agencies, and some public interest organizations. Pay attention to spring OCI options!

Tip: "If your law school does not have a big OCI program, you have to take ownership of approaching big firms either through résumé collections, alumni networking contacts, or a direct letter-writing campaign. This needs to be done in August or early September."

–Laurel A. Hajek,
Assistant Dean for Career
Services, The John Marshall
Law School, Chicago, IL

Q. I just accepted an offer with an employer, but now I see a job posting for the perfect summer job for me! What should I do?

A. Timing is everything, isn't it? You will be endlessly frustrated if you approach your job search with the thought that there's always something better just beyond the horizon. The fact is, you will always find something more appealing if you look for it. Here are some tips for dealing with buyer's remorse and its consequences:

1. There's no time like the present. When you are looking for a job—whether it's for next summer or part-time during the semester—you are searching in the moment. It sounds a bit Zen, but it's reality. Accept that your circumstances and timing are particular to this moment in your life. You can postpone doing a job search, but—again—acknowledge that by holding off until the spring of your second-year you will have foresworn interesting job openings that were available in the fall and winter.

There is no magic formula for knowing when that perfect job might appear. Moreover, there are many jobs that can offer a second-year student a good fit for the summer. Perfection is hard to attain, but a good fit—in a practice area you enjoy with people you respect and who respect you—may be as good as it gets at this stage of the game.

If you have real misgivings about an employer and your instincts tell you that you are making a bad move, listen to your gut. You are not required to accept an offer of employment. You can decline an offer politely and continue searching. Simply understand the risks and rewards of the process. You might find another job, perhaps of a better caliber. You might not. You might not want to work for a particular employer under any circumstances. That's fine, but understand the ramifications of your decision and its impact on your job search.

If you think there's another offer pending that's better than the offer in hand, you have two options:

- Ask the current employer for an extension of time to make a decision. Thus, if you have one week to decide, ask for two weeks; or

- Call the employer where you hope an offer is pending and tell them about your job offer. Sometimes the knowledge that another employer is interested in hiring you is enough to spur another employer to make a competing offer.

2. Honor deadlines and application procedures. Understand that certain job opportunities will arise and then will pass with a deadline. For instance, if you want to work for the Department of Justice in Washington, D.C. this summer, the deadline is typically very early in September.

You may think it's the perfect job, but you'll never get it if you don't adhere to the deadline. Therefore, honor the deadlines and application procedures, and be prepared. You'll miss the deadline for a plum employer if you're scrambling for an original college transcript to include in your application packet. That should have been on your radar months ago and handled prior to the start of your second summer job search.

3. Focus on the present, not what might have been. Once you accept an offer, consider yourself fortunate. You are now committed to an employer. Instead of searching for a job, traveling to interviews, and fretting about offers, you are free to focus on academics and enriching extracurricular activities. Don't mull over new job postings or consider what might have been; use your time to study, learn, and enjoy law school. Indulging in buyer's remorse will get you nowhere.

4. There's always the next job search. This job search is certainly not your last job search. There will be subsequent job searches, whether at the beginning of your third year or even earlier. Focus on the future and how to position yourself to the best of your ability in the job market. Hone your interview skills. Read up on hiring timelines and when particular opportunities are most likely to arise. Build your network of professional contacts, including alumni and mentors. Lay the foundation now so you can act from a position of knowledge and confidence.

5. Rescind an acceptance with extreme caution! Sometimes circumstances intervene that are beyond your control: a spouse must relocate, you become ill or disabled, or you are called to active duty. These are circumstances that may merit rescinding an acceptance. Consult with your career services office if you find yourself in a difficult situation. Not only is it impolite to rescind an offer, but it will also reflect poorly not only on you but on your law school. When an employer makes an offer and receives an acceptance, they have chosen you. In choosing you, they have foreclosed the chance to interview other equally qualified law students. When you retract an acceptance, you not only inconvenience an employer (they now have to start the job interview process yet again) but you breach the most basic contractual notions of offer and acceptance. You risk the prospect of being known in the wider legal community as someone who does not honor her word. Moreover, your law school will suffer because there will be guilt-by-association connected with your bad behavior. For instance, the employer may decide not to post jobs or interview at your law school for the immediate future.

Bottom line: Accept an offer with integrity and keep your word. If you are unsure about an offer, it's better to reject an offer that accept it grudgingly. Accept the Zen of the job search—live in the present circumstances. Rescind an acceptance with extreme caution.

Q. Are there special issues facing evening and part-time students during the second-year?

A. Yes. Evening and part-time students do face extra challenges—they're inevitable but not insurmountable. Because you are on campus fewer hours and have more limited time or opportunity to participate in a summer associate program, OCI may pose certain hurdles.

Should You Bother with OCI?

If you work full-time and go to school in the evenings, then you must determine if it's feasible to work as a summer associate. Will your employer allow you to take a leave of absence or use vacation time? Is this in line with your professional goals and aspirations? It may be the case that taking time off and working for a legal employer this summer is not going to work out. If that's the case, then work on alternatives to continue building experience on your law résumé.

Visit your career services office

If you do want to pursue a summer associate position either through OCI or through an independent job search, then you need to start positioning yourself with legal employers. Specifically, you ought to:

- Schedule a meeting with your career services office before fall semester classes begin.

- Bring your résumé with you and work on formatting it in a style that would be understandable to legal employers. (See page 105 for a discussion of résumés).

- Work on your job search goals and strategies.

- Rehearse your interview skills.

As an evening or part-time student, you specifically have to address the following types of questions:

- Why do you want to forego your current career and practice law?

- What motivated your decision to attend law school at this stage in you career?

- What transferable skills do you bring to this law firm?

- What legal experience do you have?

- If your graduation date will be off from the typical graduation date, be prepared to discuss this issue with a potential employer.

If you can't work this summer, you can still gain experience

If you can't find a way to take time off and devote your summer full-time to a legal job, don't despair. There are other ways to gain some experience and build your résumé. The following are some opportunities for evening or part-time students to consider:

- **Your current employer.** For part-time or evening law students, the chance to squeeze in some legal experience this summer may be an elevator ride away in your office building. Learn if your current employer has a general counsel or in-house legal department and ask about taking assignments after regular business hours or shadowing company lawyers on a day off to learn about their roles. Beyond the legal department, you're likely to find lawyers working in human resources departments (handling matters such as pensions and employee benefits) and in contract compliance departments. Short assignments or stints as a "shadow" qualify as experience if you describe them accurately on your résumé and cover letter and in your job interviews.

- **Clinics and externships.** Law school clinics, where students handle legal cases for real clients, are excellent ways to build credentials while earning academic credit. Externships are typically for-credit opportunities to work for judges, government agencies, or public interest organizations as part of the law school curriculum. Many schools will accommodate students who want to undertake clinics or externships with flexible evening and weekend hours. If your school will not make such accommodations, ask for help by petitioning the academic dean and discuss creative options with your career services counselor.

- **Research assistant positions.** Serving as a research assistant offers the chance to work closely with a faculty member, preferably in an area of practice that interests you. Research assistants proofread their professors' papers, research and update case law, and provide other support for faculty members. In some cases, research positions offer highly flexible hours.

- **Volunteer legal work.** Think about volunteering even a few hours a week after work hours with a local public interest organization or judge in order to gain some experience. Volunteering usually means you can request flexible hours, as long as you deliver on your commitment to the employer. Your legal volunteer work need not relate directly to your desired job following graduation, but at the very least it will enable you to work with lawyers and learn about the demands of serving clients.

- **Competitions.** Moot court and writing competitions also are noteworthy résumé entries. List them prominently, under a heading titled "Legal Experience," because they showcase skills in advocacy, research, and writing.

- **Law review or legal journal.** Working on a scholarly journal is much more than an academic honor—it's legal work experience. When listing this on your résumé, be sure to provide specifics about the work you do—checking cites, editing articles for substance, proofreading pages, evaluating manuscripts, and so forth. If you have administrative or managerial responsibilities, describe your work in detail. Employers will want to know how many staff members report to you, how big your budget is, how you interact with printers and other vendors, and other indications that you can thrive in an office environment.

Starting Off in a New Direction: Job Search Strategies for Second-Career Lawyers, by William A. Chamberlain, is a booklet published by NALP which discusses issues facing law students who have substantial prior career experience. Your career services office ought to have this resource.

Section 2:
Beyond On-Campus Interviewing

Most law students will find their summer jobs without the benefit of OCI. This section will discuss what students can do to deal with average grades, create a successful independent job search strategy, identify and contact employers, create networking contacts, and interview with confidence.

This section will also discuss judicial clerkships, study abroad and foreign exchange programs, long-distance job searches, public interest and non-traditional jobs, certificate and dual degree programs, and more.

Q. How should I address average or below-average grades with a potential summer employer?

A. If your grades are less than stellar, you have some roadblocks to overcome. However, grades alone will not determine your ultimate success as a lawyer. The practice of law requires intelligence, determination, attention to detail, interpersonal skills, and a wide range of other skills beyond grades.

Excellent grades—grades that place you in the top 10 percent of your class—will make you eligible for many OCI employers, federal clerkships, and particular federal agencies. However, you must couple excellent grades with strong interpersonal skills in order to be hired.

If you find yourself in the bottom half of your class, don't despair. Understand your short-term limitations and take action to improve your grades, build your résumé with meaningful work experience, and focus your long-term career goals.

Assess your Situation

First, determine why you are not performing well academically. Speak to your professors to understand whether you are missing the content, need to improve your writing skills, test-taking skills, or some combination of these. Speak to the dean of students about study skills resources, tutoring, or other academic support resources at your disposal.

Should you participate in OCI?

Participate in OCI but don't waste your time applying to highly selective employers who insist on "top 10 percent of the class." This is not a lottery and you won't slip in and get an interview because you have great interpersonal skills. If a firm definitely states their criteria and you're nowhere near the stated grades, class rank, or achievements, focus elsewhere.

Not every employer who participates in OCI wants students from the top 10 percent of the class. Many will, but some may not. Therefore, be on the lookout for the small or mid-size firm, state agency, or other employer who may come on campus in search of someone with your interests and credentials. Keep in mind, though, that relatively few, if any, smaller firms will come on campus so you cannot depend on OCI as the source of your summer job.

Q. I may be interested in a judicial clerkship, either this summer or following graduation. What do I need to know as a second-year student?

A. Second-year students can enjoy valuable work experiences during their second summer by clerking for a judge at either the local, state or federal level. Whether you work for academic credit through an externship program or are paid, you can gain experience, learn the inner workings of the court system, and forge professional connections.

While most students prefer to be paid during their second summer and might prefer a law firm job, a summer clerkship experience can be a good fit for students who need flexibility or did not succeed in securing a desired law firm job for the summer. Either way, you can build your résumé and leverage that experience going forward.

Consult judicial job postings on Symplicity and other sites through your career services office or apply directly to judges. Consult with your career services office for procedural details.

If you have plans to pursue a post-graduate clerkship, working for a judge during the summer is a great opportunity to gain experience. However, while some judges prefer to hire their previous externs, other chambers have strict rules against this procedure. Be sure to check with the judge prior to accepting an second year summer, especially if you have plans to apply to post graduate clerkships.

American Bar Association Judicial Intern Opportunity Program

http://www.abanet.org/litigation/jiop/
The Judicial Intern Opportunity Program is a full-time, six-week minimum, summer internship program open to all first- or second-year minority and/or financially disadvantaged law students who want to do legal research and writing for state or federal judges in participating cities. Participating judges are from Illinois, Texas, Miami, Phoenix, Los Angeles, San Francisco, and Washington D.C. Students may indicate geographic location preferences on their applications. Interns will receive an award of $1,500.

The program seeks to provide internship opportunities for minority or financially disadvantaged law students, those who are members of traditionally underrepresented groups in the legal profession.

Presidential Advisory Council on Diversity in the Profession

Judicial Clerkship Program, http://www.abanet.org/op/councilondiversity/jcp/home.html. A joint effort of the Advisory Council and the Judicial Division, this program is designed to bring judges and minority law students together through structured networking activities.

Students are able to demonstrate their knowledge and research skills in a small group setting while interacting with the judges in a team building effort.

Judicial Clerkships Following Graduation: Federal

Why apply for a federal clerkship following graduation? Federal clerkships offer excellent experience, prestige, and an opportunity to build a life-long mentor connection with a judge. Employers readily acknowledge the significance of a federal clerkship experience and this credential can be useful in subsequent job searches. In some cases, legal employers will offer bonuses to those who have successfully completed federal clerkships following graduation.

Your second year is the time to research judges and learn the procedural deadlines. The Online System for Clerkship Application and Review (OSCAR) has merged with the Federal Law Clerk Information System and is now the primary source of information for all federal judges and all law students seeking clerkships with federal judges following graduation. OSCAR provides the process and timeline to apply to nearly all federal judges and serves as a centralized source for judicial openings. Judges post important hiring deadlines and application requirements on OSCAR.

While the application deadline is the beginning of the fall of your third year (the exact deadline differs from year to year so research this fact), you must engage in extensive preparatory work before applying and that takes place during your second year of law school. Clerkships, like law firms, are not "one size fits all" employers. Depending upon your interests, strengths, and academic credentials, you may favor an appellate judge over a trial court judge, or visa versa. Assess your own strengths and weaknesses before making any decisions. Consult the Federal Law Clerk Hiring Plan for detailed information about deadlines during your third year.

According to Gina N. Berg, Judicial Clerkship and Project Manager at Duke Law's Career & Professional Development Center, it's important for second-year students to plan ahead. "Be aware of your law school's programs regarding clerkship opportunities, embrace the entire application process, and thoroughly research the judges," notes Berg. "Begin by identifying faculty members who can write strong letters of recommendation attesting to your writing skills and ability, as well as your personality. Judges can assess your academic strengths, but it's harder to assess your personality and 'fit' with a particular judge's chambers."

Judicial Clerkships Following Graduation: State

State court clerkships offer excellent opportunities on both the appellate and trial court levels to gain experience, research and write about interesting legal issues, and build a mentor relationship with a judge.

Unlike federal court clerkships, the procedures and timelines for state court clerkship applications are not unified. Students must research particular states and apply directly to judges. A particularly good resource for law students is *The Guide to State Judicial Clerkships,* published by Vermont Law School. It is a comprehensive guide to the procedures for applying for state court judicial clerkships at all levels in all 50 states and some U.S. territories. Your career services office ought to subscribe to *The Guide to State Judicial Clerkships.*

While many state court clerkships are not as competitive as federal court clerkships, do not let this stop you from pursuing this type of work. You can gain excellent experience, learn practical skills, and leverage those skills to a future employer.

While the clerkship application process and experience vary from state to state, it is fair to say that clerkships with a state's highest court tend to be most beneficial to your career, if you clerk where you plan to practice. For example, a clerk with the North Carolina Supreme Court not only learns local law and procedure at the state's highest level, but also earns a tremendous credential for practicing in North Carolina. Employers outside of the state in which you clerk will also recognize the general value of your judicial clerkship, regardless of whether it is at the federal or state level.

Many large law firms are offering bonuses to clerks at the highest state court equal

to those of federal clerkships. (see http://
www.lw.com/Careers.aspx?page=CareersJ
udicialClerks).

**To learn more, consider the following
judicial clerkship resources:**

Almanac of the Federal Judiciary (published
by Aspen Publishers, www.aspenpublish-
ers.com).

*BNA's Directory of State and Federal Courts,
Judges, and Clerks* (published by The Bureau
of National Affairs, Inc., www.bna.com).

*Directory of State Court Clerks & County
Courthouses* (published by CQ Press, www.
cqpress.com).

Federal-State Court Directory (published by
CQ Press, www.cqpress.com).

The Guide to State Judicial Clerkships, published by Vermont Law School, lists the application procedures, hiring timelines, and
web site information for all 50 state courts,
plus the District of Columbia, Guam, and
Puerto Rico. Also available online with a
password if your law school subscribes to
this service.

Judicial Yellow Book (published by Leadership Directories, Inc., www.leadershipdi-
rectories.com).

LEXIS/NEXIS® and WestLaw® both offer
online judicial clerkship directories. The
LEXIS/NEXIS® CourtLink database is an
important resource to consult before an in-

---

terview with a judge. CourtLink describes the types of cases a particular judge hears, as well as a calendar of proceedings, past cases that the judge has heard, and docket information.

NALP brochure, "Judicial Clerkships in Brief" (available from your career services office or www.nalp.org).

The American Bench (published by Forster-Long, Inc.)

Blogs and Websites

The following blogs and websites offer judicial clerkship information to law students. Keep in mind that blogs may not contain reliable information. Who is the author of the blog? How reliable is the source? You should not make a career decision based on a blog entry. Keep abreast of what's going on in the blogosphere, but if you have questions or a misgiving about information on the web, take your concerns to your career services office or a trusted faculty member for validation. As is the nature of blogs and web sites, this information is subject to change.

www.judicialclerkships.com offers generalized information and postings about law clerkships.

www.SoYouWantToBeaLawClerk.com offers advice to law students about the application and interview process, as well as job hunt strategies and salary information. The Clerkship Vacancies page, updated daily, provides current and upcoming clerkship opportunities. This web page also provides articles about obtaining clerkships and a FAQ page featuring reader e-mails.

www.cadc.uscourts.gov, the web site of U.S. Court of Appeals for the District of Columbia Circuit, offers a link on its home page to "Federal Judiciary Information" that may be helpful to law students. In addition, **http://www.cadc.uscourts.gov/internet/lawclerk.nsf/Home?OpenForm** offers FAQs about the federal judges law clerk hiring plan.

Check out FindLaw's Greedy Clerks web board: **http://www.infirmation.com/bboard/clubs.tcl?topic=Greedy%20Clerks.**

The Clerkship Notification Blog can be found at **http://lawschoolclerkship.blogspot.com/.** One of the blog administrators writes that, "the goal of this blog is to provide a forum for law clerk applicants to share information regarding their clerkship applications. By using the 'comments' function, applicants can easily find and share information as to which judges have started calling applicants, which judges have started making offers, and which judges have completed their hiring."

http://lawclerkaddict.blogspot.com/ is a blog that, according to its administrator, provides "information about which prestigious law schools send clerks to feeder or other federal circuit court of appeals judges."

http://scotuslawclerkplacement.blogspot.com/ discusses U.S. Supreme Court clerkship hires and offers application advice.

For general information about the members of the federal judiciary, see Underneath their Robes at **http://underneaththeirrobes.blogs.com/** and Above the Law at **www.abovethelaw.com**.

Considering a judicial clerkships following graduation?

- Start early with your research and fact-finding. First semester of your second year is a good time to start to think about a post-graduate clerkship and identifying particular courts and geographic locales that truly interest you.

- Consult your career services office for procedures, timelines, and resources specific to your law school. Your law school may have a staff professional dedicated solely to judicial clerkships who can offer advice and expertise.

- Clerk for the value of the experience, not merely the prestige. You need to truly enjoy research and writing on a day-to-day basis. Otherwise, your clerkship experience will be an extremely miserable year in your life.

- Follow the timeline and procedures. The deadlines for federal clerkships are very strict.

- Be realistic about matching your credentials to a particular court or

---

judge. You will find the right "fit" for your skills and interests.

- In the spring semester of your second year, you should be hearing about law clerkship education programs through your career services office. If you are not aware of a program, visit your career services office and start the process yourself.

- Identify faculty members who can write strong letters of recommendation.

- Connect with faculty and third-year students for advice.

If you're thinking about career moves after law school, consider the following advice:

Judicial clerkships are not solely the domain of recent law school graduates. For some, a judicial clerkship position can be a full-time career track after you gain a few years of experience with a firm, government agency, or public interest organization. These types of professional law clerk positions offer excellent experience and reasonable hours in a challenging intellectual environment.

Therefore, if you need to work for a law firm in order to pay off student loan debt or simply don't see the point of clerking directly after law school, know that a growing number of judges will hire lawyers with a few years' experience. Sometimes the hires occur because of a sudden vacancy on the judges' staff, an increase in docketed cases, or the desire to move away from temporary law clerks to a more full-time law clerk model.

Another opportunity besides a law clerk assigned to a particular judge is to work as a staff attorney for a particular circuit or court system. In many jurisdictions, lawyers work as law clerks to all the judges in a particular court system, drafting and researching on particular issues, or being assigned to particular judges as circumstances dictate.

The processes for hiring full-time law clerks with experience and staff attorneys are not handled through OSCAR and may be found in bar association newsletters or word-of-mouth.

Q. How important are extracurricular activities to employers?

A. Be careful about overloading your schedule and your résumé with extracurricular activities. Balance your academic life with one or two activities that truly highlight your interests. Using extracurricular activities to offset poor grades will not benefit you. Practice moderation when participating in extracurricular activities and focus on academic excellence and developing a strong network of professional connections.

Here's what one successful professional has to say: "Academic excellence is what will get you in the door," observes Melissa Brill, a member of Cozen O'Connor in New York City. "Hiring decisions at larger firms are based primarily on grades and law school ranking. Although you shouldn't devote yourself to extracurricular activities at the expense of your academic performance, an unusual or interesting activity on your résumé is a great conversation starter and can make you more memorable. It may also be a great way to learn and network."

Q. How can I find a public interest job this summer?

A. Public interest law includes a variety of different employment sectors: non-profit organizations, non-government organizations (NGOs), government agencies, think tanks, and special interest organizations. Public interest encompasses a broad spectrum of interests and ideals; many people mistakenly think of public interest lawyers as left-of-center hippie types. In fact, you will find lawyers from across the political spectrum in various non-profit organizations, think tanks, and special interest organizations. The unifying denominator of public interest organizations is that they serve the public interest (depending on how you define public interest) and are typically non-profit operations.

Finding full-time work in the public interest sector is among the most challenging hurdles facing recent graduates. Contrary to some misconceptions about public interest law (ever hear a classmate say, "I'll find a job with a public interest organization if I can't find a 'real' job"?), you need to build your public interest résumé from the day you set foot in law school.

If you're committed to working full-time in public interest law following graduation, then you may want to consider working in the public interest arena during your second summer. This may be easier said than done. Many public interest organizations cannot afford to pay a salary to law students or if they can pay a salary, it is typically very low. While your law school may have summer grants to help students working in the public interest field, it's still a challenge.

In addition, public interest organizations require a high level of commitment as evidenced on your résumé and in your interview. You need to demonstrate to public interest organizations that you have a proven track record in the public interest world, whether through paid work or a history of volunteering for like-minded causes. Your cover letter, too, must demonstrate your firm commitment to public interest law.

If you have the desire (and the credentials) to work at a large firm as a summer associate this summer but are considering a full-time public interest career sometime after you graduate, keep in mind that many large law firms now offer public interest or pro bono opportunities for summer associates. You should research this information well in advance of OCI, preferably in July or August before your second year begins. Finding a large law firm that provides pro bono or public interest opportunities during the summer enables you to have the best of both worlds—for-profit experience at a big firm coupled with the ability to be of service to underserved populations. For more information about positioning yourself for a public interest job following graduation, see page 83.

Enlist the help of your law school career services office. There are many resources specific to particular law schools, including summer grant money, that you need to know about. In addition, some law schools have specialized public interest law staff professionals who work solely on public interest jobs. If you attend a law school with such services, consider yourself fortunate and take advantage of these opportunities. If your law school has more limited offerings, consider these resources:

PSLawNet

The best source for public interest law opportunities can be found at PSLawNet (www.pslawnet.org), the National Association for Law Placement's Public Service Law Network Worldwide. PSLawNet is a network of over 170 law schools and more than 11,000 law-related public interest organizations in the U.S. and around the world.

Through its online database, PSLawNet offers a comprehensive clearinghouse of public interest organizations and opportunities for law students. Users can perform customized searches of public interest opportunities around the world, ranging from short-term volunteer and paid internships to full-time jobs, fellowships and pro bono opportunities.

Equal Justice Works

In addition to helping encourage the next generation of public interest lawyers, Equal Justice Works (www.equaljusticeworks.org) offers two services of interest to second-year students:

Conference and Career Fair

Each year, Equal Justice Works hosts the largest national public service job fair at its Conference and Career Fair. The event typically attracts more than 1,000 law students and graduates, as well as more than 150 public interest employers—national nonprofit organizations, public defenders, legal aid offices and federal government agencies—seeking to fill internships and staff positions in public interest law.

Summer Internships

Summer Corps is an Equal Justice Works AmeriCorps program that in 2007 provided 350 law students with a $1,000 education award for spending the summer using their legal skills on behalf of low-income individuals, families and communities who would otherwise not have access to justice. Summer Corps members provide critically needed legal services, increase the staffing capacity of the nonprofit organizations where they work, and build the resources of the community-based organizations with whom they collaborate.

Bar association resources

Many bar associations, from national entities such as the American Bar Association to your local bar association, offer summer internship programs for law students. These types of opportunities might entail research into specific issues ranging from international treaties to planning continuing legal education programs. For instance, the American Bar Association Law Student Division recently listed the following summer internship opportunities on their web site (www.abanet.org/lsd):

- The Janet D. Steiger Fellowship Project offers first- and second-year law students the opportunity for summer work in the Consumer Protection Departments and/or Antitrust Law Departments of state attorneys general offices throughout the United States. The ABA Section of Antitrust Law provides each participant with a stipend.

- Asian Law Initiative offers student fellowships and internships.

- Central European and Eurasian Law Initiative (CEELI), a public service project of the ABA, offers law student internships in order to advance the rule of law by supporting the law reform process in Central and Eastern Europe and the former Soviet Union.

- The ABA Commission on Law and Aging offers seasonal internships designed to provide law students interested in pursing a career focusing on law and aging issues with experience in a nationally known organization in that field.

- The ABA Division for Public Services provides summer internships designed to allow students to participate in public interest legal research and writing project during a 10-week period. Areas of involvement include bioethics and the law, disability law, election law, environmental law, homelessness, poverty, immigration law, national security law, and substance abuse.

- The Curtin Justice Fund Legal Internship Program seeks law students willing to spend the summer working for a bar association or legal services program designed to prevent homelessness or assist homeless or indigent clients or their advocates. The Commission on Homelessness and Poverty Legal Internship Program provides legal assistance to organizations serving the under-represented and gives students direct experience in a public interest forum.

Another ABA resource is the ABA Standing Committee on Pro Bono and Public Interest Law (http://www.abanet.org/legalservices/probono/home.html).

National Legal Aid and Defender Association, www.nlada.org, is a helpful resource for those interested in public defense and legal aid job opportunities.

Clinic opportunities

Your law school may allow second-year students to spend the summer working for a clinic. Research your law school's clinical offerings and see if this option works for you. Clinics enable law students to meet and help live clients, research legal issues, and—in some instances—prepare for hearings, trials, or depositions.

Q. I want to work in public interest law following graduation. What steps should I take during second year to secure a job in this area after graduation?

A. Public interest law is among the most challenging sectors of law in which to find employment, particularly full-time employment following graduation. According to NALP employment statistics, only between 2 and 3 percent of all law graduates find jobs in the public interest sector directly following graduation. This can be explained in a few ways:

- There are few entry-level openings in public interest law (most vacancies are hired from the ranks of more experienced attorneys);

- Some graduates who may be destined for public interest law are hired first as judicial clerks directly following law school and this skews the numbers; and

- Low salary levels and high student loan debt combine to make public interest law a choice that lawyers can afford to make only after working in the private sector for several years and stabilizing themselves financially.

In order to maximize your ability to work in the public interest sector following graduation, here are some tips to position yourself to succeed:

1. Build your résumé with solid public interest law experience. Include public interest extracurricular activities or jobs that you held in college that demonstrate your commitment to a particular cause or population. For your first summer job, try to find something in the public sector to build your law school résumé credentials. Public interest employers value seeing someone who demonstrates a long-term commitment through deed and word.

2. Participate in extracurricular activities that further establish your public interest credentials. While you should not ignore academic performance, do find a one or two well-selected extracurricular venues for you to shine. For instance, learn more about PSLawNet or Equal Justice Works, locate the public interest/pro bono subcommittee at your local bar association and get involved, and work with your law school administration to support law students choosing public interest careers.

3. Find big law firms that support public interest and pro bono work. If you are choosing to work for a large law firm this summer, try to find a firm that offers pro bono activities and demonstrates a strong commitment to serving underserved populations. You can have the best of both worlds: big firm summer associate experience coupled with a meaningful pro bono component. This type of experience will further build your résumé and your credibility with public interest employers.

4. Participate in a law school clinic. Consider taking a clinic during the second semester of your second year or during your third year. Clinics typically serve indigent populations and enable you to gain practical experience and build credentials.

5. Opt for an independent study project. If your schedule is really constricted (either because you've registered for so many classes or you are an evening or part-time student), consider taking on an independent study project that focuses on a public interest subject or population. This way, you can earn credits, create a larger network, and develop your résumé so that it interests a public interest employer.

6. Deal with student loan debt issues now. Among the biggest obstacles to finding a job in the public interest sector is the harsh reality that a public interest law job may have a $42,000 annual salary but your combined college and law school student loans now total $100,000. What can you do? The following options will help you fulfill your ultimate dream of working in public interest law:

- Find out if your school offers a loan repayment assistance program, public interest scholarships, or other incentives to law students who want to pursue public sector law following graduation.

- Research scholarship opportunities for third year in order to lessen student loan debt.

- Save now for the career you want later. The more money you have saved (and the less debt you incur in law school), the more choices you have following graduation. Therefore, make smart financial decisions and live frugally now so you can serve the public later.

- Explore loan repayment plans (federal, state and local), loan consolidation plans, and other ways to lessen or eliminate loan repayment obligations.

Q. How do I find a job abroad this summer? Is there still a chance to participate in a summer study abroad experience as a second-year or is that not advisable? Are there other options for students seeking study abroad experience?

A. Summer study versus semester abroad

In most instances, summer study abroad may not be the best choice for this summer; it's more important to gain some practical experience in the U.S. However, this does not mean that a summer study experience has passed you by forever. "Not all study abroad is summer-based," says Louis Thompson, Assistant Dean for Graduate and International Programs at Temple University Beasley School of Law. "If you could not participate in a study abroad experience during your first summer, consider a semester-long study abroad program during your second- or third-year of law school."

More law schools are offering semester abroad opportunities for upper-class students. For instance, Temple University Beasley School of Law has a campus in Tokyo, Japan and the Tokyo program is open to non-Temple students. The curriculum focuses on international business law and between 30% and 40% of students work on internships with Japanese businesses or firms during the semester or in the summer following.

Semester abroad timing issues

If you are a second-year student contemplating a semester study abroad program, then be aware of deadlines. In many cases, you need to complete application materials by October in anticipation of spring semester study. This means that you have to multi-task during OCI.

Moreover, some study abroad opportunities take place in the fall of your second year. This means that you may have to miss OCI or you must take action to complete your interviews before you depart on your semester abroad. It's challenging, but it can be done with careful planning.

Exchange programs—Another option
In addition to study abroad through an ABA-accredited law school, some U.S. law schools arrange semester-long exchange programs with foreign law schools. What is difference between a semester abroad program and an exchange program? A semester abroad program is run by a U.S. law school and you study with other American law students. On an exchange program, you are studying with foreign students at a foreign law school and your credits transfer back to your home law school.

If your law school does not have a semester study abroad or exchange program with a foreign law school, research other law schools because they often accept law students from elsewhere in the U.S. It's up to you to arrange the transfer of credits to fulfill your graduation requirements.

Do you want to practice international business law?
"If you want to be an international business lawyer, you give yourself more value if you practice in the U.S. for a period of time fol-

lowing graduation," advises Thompson of Temple University. "Foreign lawyers will ask, 'what are you bringing to the table?' Gaining experience in American business law here in the states before going abroad may help build your credentials. Therefore, take the job as a summer associate and get a few years of commercial law experience under your belt before taking your career to the next level."

Do you want to practice international human rights law?

"If you are public-interest minded and want to practice in the area of international human rights law, it may be worthwhile for you to travel abroad during your second summer and do work in that area. Public interest lawyers value the experience and demonstrated commitment to a particular cause. Therefore, consider traveling abroad this summer and getting an internship with a human rights organization—it's worthwhile. Some students have deferred their graduation in order to work for the International War Crimes Tribunal in Rwanda—that's how important it is to 'walk the walk' in public interest law."

International law resources

Three especially helpful resources in the area of international law are:

- The American Society of International Law (www.asil.org) publishes information about international internship opportunities that is very comprehensive. Click on "Resources" and then go to "Career Development" for internship information.

- *Serving the Public: A Job Search Guide, Volume II—International,* published by Harvard Law School includes an extensive listing of over 400 potential employers. In also contains updated fellowship, summer funding and bibliography information, new information on international work on Capitol Hill, international litigation, development work, and opportunities for international positions in state or local government.

- The ABA Section of International Law Student Headquarters (http://www.abanet.org/intlaw/students/home.html) is a very good educational website geared toward both the study of international law and in educating students about pathways to international practice. It also contains good information on international law internships.

Tips for students interested in study abroad and international law

- Research study abroad opportunities at your law school and other law schools. It's not too late to study abroad!

- Timing is everything. Keep in mind that study abroad may interfere with OCI or require that you be proactive about contacting employers. Know the risks and rewards before you proceed. It may be the case that you ought to work at a firm this summer

---

and defer an exchange program until your third year. Speak to your career services office for guidance.

- If you want to practice in international public interest law, such as human rights, it may be worthwhile for you to skip OCI and find an internship in that area this summer either in the U.S. or abroad.

- If you are focused on international business law, take all the international law classes you can, but consider staying in the U.S. this summer, gaining experience in American law, and starting your career in the U.S. Generally speaking, experience in U.S. law will be an important credential for foreign lawyers seeking our advice.

Q. I'm interested in a non-traditional career path. How do I find these jobs? Even if I ultimately want to work in a non-traditional venue after graduation, should I nonetheless work in a traditional legal job during my second summer?

A. Non-traditional legal careers encompass a wide range of choices, from banking and finance to human resources and sports management. You will find law graduates in nearly every sector of the business market enjoying satisfying and successful career paths.

Why are non-traditional careers so alluring? First, for many law graduates the day-to-day practice of law fails to offer career satisfaction and work-life balance, or conflicts with their personal and professional desires. Many lawyers who do not practice law will tell you that law school as an educational experience was immensely satisfying yet they envisioned a different career path from traditional practice.

Some law students arrive at law school knowing they will seek a non-traditional career path. Others arrive at the decision to work in a non-legal venue either during law school or several years following graduation. Either way, you should consider your options carefully when contemplating this decision, particularly when contemplating your second summer job.

"Second-year students contemplating a non-traditional career path should ask themselves, 'What's making me say this? What's driving this decision?'" remarks Cheryl Rich Heisler, president and founder of LAWTER-NATIVES™, and author of the forthcoming edition of *What Can You Do With a Law Degree?*, published by DecisionBooks.

Heisler suggests that law students contemplating an alternative career path begin by performing a self-assessment of one's skills and interests. Ask yourself:

- What do you like to do? For instance, what are your hobbies or extracurricular pursuits?

- What did people think about you? For instance, go back to your high school or college yearbooks and see what people wrote about you.

- What were the best jobs you ever had? Explain why they were great jobs.

- What would you do if you won the lottery?

- What are your long-terms goals?

Work with your career services office and seek advice, mentoring, and support. Understand that your second summer employment record can help or hinder your entrance into a non-traditional career path. "If you're unsure about whether to take the nontraditional route after graduation, take the opportunity during your second summer to work in a traditional legal environment," advises Heisler. "The traditional legal work gives you credibility and enables you to see, once and for all, if law is right for you. Don't foreclose the opportunity to get that experience on your record."

Some law students had unpleasant first summer jobs in the legal field and are questioning their decision to practice law following graduation. This is not unusual and you need to address these concerns by working in a legal venue. "If you had a bad work experience during your first summer, don't let one bad work episode taint the waters for traditional legal practice," advises Heisler.

Conversely, if you absolutely, positively know that you do not want to practice law, view your second summer as an opportunity to gain practice experience in your area of interest. "If you know you don't want to practice law and are seeking an alternative career postgraduation, you need to find a job that relates to what you are interested in doing with your career," notes Carla DeVelder, director of the Notre Dame Law School Career Services Office. "If you are interested in higher education administration, find a position with your university or law school in the admissions, student services, or career services office. If you are interested in writing for a career, you must start publishing now. You need to use your second summer to make connections, become known in the industry, and bring to the table some of that experience that everyone wants and needs you to have."

Heisler echoes these sentiments: "For those students who are convinced that nontraditional is the route to pursue, go get the experience and skills in your area of interest. Use that experience to weave together a compel-

ling story for marketing yourself to a nontraditional employer during your third year. For
instance, if you truly want to work in non-
profit management and use your law degree
in a nontraditional way, then take concrete
steps to find work in that sector during your
second summer and start building your credentials."

Suggested reading:

Nonlegal Careers for Lawyers by Gary A. Mun-
neke, William D. Henslee, and Ellen Wayne
(5th ed., ABA).

One Person/Multiple Careers by Marci Alboher
(Warner Business Books).

What Can You Do With a Law Degree? by Cheryl
Rich Heisler (6th ed., DecisionBooks)

Q. Is it true that I have to pick a practice area specialty during law school? I feel pressure to choose a specific career path and don't know what to do.

A. A law degree is a graduate degree that is general in nature; there is no need to specialize while you are in law school unless you feel compelled to do so. A J.D. degree is like an M.D. degree in the sense that it is a general graduate degree. A doctor receives a comprehensive education in order to become licensed in a particular state. Specializing in the medical profession occurs after graduation through residency and fellowship programs. Similarly, a law degree enables you to sit for the bar exam in a particular jurisdiction and practice law. Specialization tends to occur after one graduates and begins working full-time.

During law school you may be tempted to follow "hot" practice area trends and gear your studies in a particular direction through certificate or dual degree programs. Many legal publications will tout "hot" practice areas and predict what specialties will be in demand. Be cautious about following the latest practice trends. What may be "hot" this year, may cool down by the time you graduate. Also keep in mind that forcing yourself to practice in an area that does not play to your strengths or interests will fail in the long-run. Better to gain a broad legal education, sample different practice areas though work experiences or classes, and present yourself to employers as a person with a range of interests.

If you are inclined to focus on a particular practice area, consider these tips:

- Take courses in your area of interest. If you are truly interested in a particular practice area, then law school is the time to take as many courses as possible in that area. If there are graduate courses offered by other schools, such as the graduate school of business, public policy, or international affairs, then explore the options and see if you can cross-register and take those courses. Arming yourself with knowledge, connections, and evidence of your commitment to a particular practice area will inure to your benefit as you build your résumé.

- Gain practical experience. There is no substitute for practical experience, whether paid, volunteer or for academic credit, in your area of interest. Experience not only tells a potential employer that you are genuinely interested in that practice specialty, but you were willing to go forth and get the experience in that area. Experience is also important because it can help you decide if your ideal practice area is truly a good fit for you. Test the waters and do not rely on television or movies to influence your career choice. Too often students arrive at law school convinced that they want to be federal prosecutors only to find out that they either do not like being in a court room or have no interest in the criminal justice system. Better to figure this out now than later.

- Network and conduct informational interviews. One of the best ways to test your theories is to meet practitioners and ask questions first-hand. By tapping into your school's alumni network or conducting your own research, you can find practitioners and see for yourself if a career as a real estate lawyer is right for you. For a full discussion of networking and informational interviewing, see page 145.

- Consider having two résumés. Have one for a specific practice area of interest and another for more generalized practice opportunities. This way, you can market yourself to lawyers practicing in specialty areas and promote your relevant accomplishments and have a more generalized résumé for other employers that may be of interest.

Tip: Be careful about promoting an interest in sports and entertainment law or international law. Both practice areas are notoriously difficult to break into and are quite dependent on geography. While you

---

will find lawyers with international practices in Des Moines, you are much more likely to find international lawyers in large metropolitan areas. Therefore, if you want to live and work in a smaller metropolitan area (or a rural area), consider carefully how you are going to promote your credentials and interests to an employer.

Focusing unduly on a desire to practice sports and entertainment law or international law also may signal to a potential employer that you may have unrealistic expectations about practicing law. The small firm specializing in civil trial practice may want to interview you but will think twice if your résumé seems too focused on areas that are not practiced by that firm.

To learn more about practice area specialties, read *The Official Guide to Legal Specialties: An Insider's Guide to Every Major Practice Area* by Lisa L. Abrams (Harcourt, 2000).

Q. I attend law school on the East Coast but want to work on the West Coast this summer. How do I manage a long-distance job search?

A. Long-distance job searches can be frustrating and time-consuming experiences. There are ways, however, to ease the difficulties and create a strategy that can work for you. Here are some tips and ideas to guide you:

- **Start the job search process early.** As a second-year law student looking for a summer job from a distance, you should begin the process early. In fact, if you are spending your first summer in the city where you would ultimately like to end up next summer, it's an efficient use of your time and an employer's resources to interview you—at least preliminarily—before you return to school for your second year. Many large firm employers and federal agencies are willing to begin the interview process before your second year classes begin, so definitely reach out to employers during your first summer and see if interviews can be arranged before school begins.

- **Research thoroughly.** Where would you like to work? Is it a large city with a very competitive job market? How many law schools are located in that market? What's the economy like? Are there job fairs scheduled? If it's a very competitive job market, are there alternatives nearby? For instance, Manhattan is a very popular destination for lawyers and a very competitive one. If you are committed to being in New York City, what alternatives exist? Would you be willing to work in one of the other boroughs? Northern New Jersey? Connecticut? Spend the time to learn the market.

- **Get reciprocity to use another law school's career services office.** If you want to know another market thoroughly, then consider getting reciprocity to use another law school's career services office. You can do this by visiting your career services office and making the request. Keep in mind that getting reciprocity sometimes takes time, particularly in very popular employment markets, so plan ahead and be patient. Reciprocity varies from school to school: in some cases, you have access to all job posting and services. In other instances, you only have access to postings.

- **Connect-the-dots, particularly in smaller markets.** Be prepared to explain to potential employers why you want to live in a particular city, particularly smaller cities and rural areas. Few people will question your desire to live in the large metropolitan areas such as New York, Chicago, Los Angeles, and the like. However, you will need to make a case to employers—particularly if it's not readily apparent from your résumé—that you want to relocate to a smaller city or rural area.

- **Network.** If you are conducting a long-distance job search, it helps to have allies on location to help you. This is where alumni connections (college and law school) can help you. In addition, consider joining the local bar association as a law student member in order to tap into job postings, learn the latest news, and establish your sincere interest in the area. For a detailed discussion of networking, see page 145.

- **Schedule travel time to your intended destination.** If you are truly committed to relocating following graduation and want to interview for summer jobs in that city, then schedule travel time to your intended destination. Try to schedule travel time during vacations; however, you may find it expeditious to schedule travel time to interview with employers during school time. Mention that you have specific travel time in your cover letter. Use your good judgment and do not simply travel for informational interviews, but definitely avail yourself of interview opportunities if you are truly committed to a particular city or region.

Should You Visit Another Law School During Your Third Year?

Looking ahead to third-year—should you apply for visiting status at another law school? If you are really serious about relocating to a distant locale following graduation, then consider becoming a visiting student at a law school close to your intended destination. You attend law school in the market where you want to ultimately work, but receive your diploma from your "home" law school. You must speak with your dean of students and career services office in order to start the process. For some law students, this can be a good solution because it enables you to network extensively and you can apply for part-time jobs in order to build your résumé with local connections. The disadvantage to visiting, for some students, is that you lose your sense of connectivity to your classmates (if this is important to you) and you may be considered a second-class citizen at your visiting school because your are not considered a graduate of that school.

Section 3:
Packaging Yourself for Employers

A successful job search process involves presenting yourself to employers in a manner that showcases your credentials in the best possible light. This includes drafting a great résumé, writing a cogent cover letter, demonstrating savvy interview skills, networking abilities, and insuring that your Internet face is employer-friendly.

Q. What does a law school résumé look like?

A. A law résumé is a unique document that differs from a business school résumé or an academic curriculum vitae or "CV." Legal employers expect to see your information in a particular format.

A law résumé lists relevant experiences, typically in reverse chronological order using three or four main headings: CONTACT INFORMATION, EDUCATION, EXPERIENCE, AND OTHER (optional). There is no "Objective" or "Goal" at the top of a law résumé. Your goal or objective is to find a legal job; everyone knows this. Your cover letter is the place where you will articulate your goals and objectives for a prospective employer (see page 127 for a discussion of cover letters).

> **Tip:** Avoid templates, such as Résumé Wizard, readily available on most word processing programs. Templates severely limit your ability to manipulate your information and move text around to make it fit. Most templates are designed, not to maximize space, but to appear pretty. You don't need pretty. You need information conveyed in an easy-to-read format.

To reiterate, your résumé consists of—in the following order:

- CONTACT INFORMATION
- EDUCATION
- EXPERIENCE

· OTHER (optional)

Contact Information

This information appears at the very top of your résumé and comprises your:

· Name
· Mailing address (where you can be reached reliably)
· Telephone number (ditto)
· E-mail address

An employer needs to know what to call you, and how to reach you by regular mail, e-mail, and phone. Pretty straightforward, really. Nonetheless, there are some issues worth addressing here:

Name

First name, middle initial, last name
Example: Emily J. Smith

If your name is non-specific with regard to your gender (either it is gender neutral, like Brett or Rivers) or foreign, you might want to consider appending a Mr. or Ms. in front of your name in parentheses just to tip off an employer as to how to address you properly. It's only fair. This way, you won't be outraged when you receive a rejection letter addressed to "Mr. Porjatu Miller" and you're a woman. Save the righteous indignation for the times when you signal quite clearly that you're female (or male) and the employer fails to get the hint.

Mailing address

Ideally, your mailing address should be the location where your incoming mail will be safeguarded and not misplaced by irresponsible roommates or ill-behaved pets. In most cases, it should be your place of residence where you can get mail and respond promptly.

Tip: If you are seeking employment in a particular city and want to establish a connection that may not be apparent from your résumé, consider having a "School Address" or "Current Address" as well as a second listing, "Home Address." This dual address system is particularly relevant for employers in smaller cities and towns. You don't necessarily need to establish a connection with employers in cities such as New York, Washington, D.C., Chicago, Los Angeles, Boston, or San Francisco, but smaller cities often favor those who demonstrate a legitimate local tie. A dual address at the top of your résumé conveys to an employer that you have a connection to the area. Thus, if you're going to school in Washington, D.C. and attended college in Boston, but desperately want to return home to Columbus, you may want to add two items to your résumé: a "Home Address" with your parents' address (or a close relative's) and a reference to your high school to the Education section.

Telephone number. List the phone number where you can be reached reliably. Many law students list both their apartment phone number and their cell phone.

- If you have roommates, instruct them about the importance of answering the phone civilly and taking accurate messages. You really don't want to come home to a message, scrawled like a ransom note, that says: "Lawyer called. Call back."

- If you have an answering machine or voicemail at home or on your cell phone, make sure your message is professional and consistent with the lawyerly image you want to convey. The days of loud music blaring in the background with the message, "We're out partying! Leave a message for Bill and if I'm not completely drunk, I'll call ya back ..." are over. Now is the time to have the following message recorded in a clear, confident voice, "You have reached the phone number of (your name here). I am not available at this time. Please leave a message and I will return your call as soon as possible. Thank you."

- Check your messages regularly, particularly when your résumé is in play. At least three times a day, check your voicemail to make sure you haven't missed any calls.

- Return calls promptly, preferably the same business day.

- If you are dealing with time zone changes, take a moment and calculate whether you're calling during office hours.

E-mail address. Many lawyers prefer to e-mail rather than call, so list an e-mail address at the top of your résumé.

- Check your e-mail regularly and respond promptly.

- Make sure your e-mail address is entirely professional. Avoid having suggestive e-mail addresses; it shows poor judgment.

- When writing responses to e-mails, keep your correspondence professional.

- No emoticans (smiley faces or other graphics).

- Avoid provocative quotes at the end of your e-mails; save those for your friends and family. A prospective employer does not need to know that you are quoting Mao or Che Guevera as the "signature" to your e-mail.

- Beware of links on your e-mail responses to a personal web site or blog that may be self-incriminating.

- Keep your e-mail "signatures" simple: Your name, address, and telephone number.

Education

This information should appear in reverse chronological order (most recent first); therefore, begin with law school. Give your law school (bolded), city, your degree, and your projected date of graduation. As a second-year law student, this is the relevant information to share. It ought to look like this:

University of Pennsylvania School of Law, Philadelphia, PA
J.D. expected, May 2010

The degree you are earning is a J.D. or, more fully, a Juris Doctor degree. **There is no such thing as a Juris Doctorate.**

You should also list relevant information beneath your law school entry pertaining to academic achievement honors. For instance, do list:

- Awards
- Honors
- Grade point average
- Class rank
- Dual degree
- Evening division
- Certificate programs
- Scholarships
- Law review or journal
- Extracurricular activities
- Study abroad experiences

Other graduate degrees

Beneath your law school entry, you should list the last degree you earned. If you already earned an M.B.A., Ph.D., or M.A., that information goes here. For example:

Harvard University, Cambridge, MA
M.A. in Comparative Literature,
cum laude, May 2004
Thesis: "19th Century Russian Poetry: The St. Petersburg Society"

Undergraduate degree

Next, in order, list your undergraduate degree. If you transferred schools, list the school where you earned your degree. Similarly, if you earned an A.A. degree from a junior college or community college, skip this information and list the school where you earned your bachelor's degree. Students who transferred to different schools or took time off might have two, three or more undergraduate entries. Detail becomes confusing and offers too much information. Keep it relevant and tell the employer where you finally earned your undergraduate degree, the degree earned, and the year which you earned it. For example:

University of Chicago, Chicago, IL
B.A. in History, May 2005

Relevant information to add to the entry about your undergraduate degree includes:

- Grade point average
- Class rank (if available or applicable)
- Honors
- Scholarships
- Awards
- Study abroad experience
- Theses and independent research projects
- Extracurricular activities

Here is why each of these entries may be relevant to a prospective employer:

- **Grade point average (GPA)** conveys your level of academic achievement. If you earned over a 3.0, furnish your GPA. If you had an overall GPA below 3.0 but achieved over a 3.0 in your major, you can list that information. For example: Major GPA: 3.7. This signals to an employer that you have achieved academically in particular discipline.

Tip: Many students who do not perform well in law school do not list their grades or class rank under the law school section. The students also remove GPA information from their undergraduate section. The theory, they explain, is that they don't want to call attention to the fact that they are not academic stars in law school. A related theory is that they want everything on the résumé to be "symmetrical." This is misguided. If your law school grades are mediocre, then it's all the more reason to emphasize that you achieved academically in college! Give employers tangible evidence that you are smart, motivated, and successful academically. When you list your undergraduate grades and neglect to list your law school grades, the general understanding is: "Here's a person who has the capacity to do well academically." When you don't list any information about your grades, employers are left wondering if you have distinguished yourself in any way whatsoever. Provide relevant information and be prepared to discuss grades (see page 63 for a full discussion).

- **Class rank (if available).** If your college provided you with a class rank and you placed well in your class (top 25%), list this information as an indication of your academic success. Along with GPA, class rank information offers evidence of your academic achievement relative to your classmates. This can be particularly important if you went to a small college that may not be well-known. Graduating first in your class from a small, local college may carry additional weight with employers who may not know the school.

- **Honors.** If your school conferred the Latin honors *cum laude, magna cum laude,* or *summa cum laude,* list these—as illustrated above—in all lower case letters and italicized. If your college conferred honors, high honors, or departmental honors, list these accordingly. Bottom line: convey to an employer that you did well and list this information prominently and unambiguously.

- **Scholarships.** If you received scholarships to attend college, list these. Some scholarships are merit-based, others are based on financial need. Receipt of a scholarship means you were identified as a promising student worthy of financial support.

- **Awards.** List relevant academic awards such as Phi Beta Kappa, as well as any alumni/ae awards, leadership, and service awards.

- **Study abroad experience.** If you studied abroad, this experience is worthy to share in a line or two. This information conveys that you have a broader experience beyond your campus and may have a larger world-view (no guarantee, but sometimes these perceptions are important).

- **Theses and independent research projects.** Lawyers value research and writing skills highly; these skills are essential to professional success. Therefore, giving employers information about a thesis or independent research project offers relevant evidence of your ability to study a subject, perform independent research, and write clearly. List the title of your thesis or independent research project and be prepared to discuss this information in your interview.

- **Extracurricular activities.** Limit extracurricular activities to those where you took a leadership role. Long, exhaustive lists of every committee or subcommittee on which you served won't help you. For example, if you belonged to a fraternity or sorority, list your membership and any substantive leadership positions you held. Don't list a paragraph of activities beginning with "Spring Carnival, Clean-Up Committee Co-Chair." Ask yourself, "Is this information relevant to an employer?" If it does not pass muster, then don't list it. If the substance of the activity is not readily apparent to an unknowing reader from name alone, explain the activity.

Take a look at the following example of a more fully described undergraduate résumé listing:

University of Chicago, Chicago, IL
B.A. in History, *summa cum laude,*
May 2005
GPA: 3.8/4.0

Honors and Awards: Dean's List (2002-2005), Alumni Merit Scholarship recipient (2001-2005), Phi Beta Kappa, Best Undergraduate Thesis (2005)

Thesis: "Post-European Colonialism in Africa: Zimbabwe's Journey to Independence"

Activities: Undergraduate History Club, Women's Intramural Rowing Club, Chicago Road Runners (distance running club)

Study Abroad: Cambridge University, King's College (spring semester, 2003)

Experience

Experience on a legal résumé is typically listed in reverse chronological order, with the most recent job listed first. Some law résumés also divide the EXPERIENCE category into two sub-headings: LEGAL EXPERIENCE and OTHER EXPERIENCE. This is a matter of preference based on the nature of your prior experience.

As a second-year student, you ought to have at least one legal experience from your prior summer. Showcase this information and highlight the specific skills you mastered: research, analysis, and writing.

Because the legal profession is, at its core, a client service industry, focus on the service aspects of other jobs you have held. Whether you worked as a camp counselor, waiter or waitress, in retail, or any other typical college job, begin by listing your title, the experience, and dates of work (month and year is sufficient or even the semester and year; you need not list the day you started and the day you ended). When describing the experience, don't puff. It's okay if you didn't launch an Internet start-up, run a real estate conglomerate, or cure AIDS. Employers will see through the puffing.

In terms of formatting, find a style that works for you. Some people like to lead with the title and bold that information. Others prefer to lead with the employer name (particularly if the employer is well known) and provide that information first. Some people prefer the paragraph method (indent and list sentences in order). Others prefer bullet points. The paragraph system uses space more efficiently. Bullet points are a great way to use space if you don't have much to say at this point.

The following is an example of a typical entry in two versions (paragraph style versus bullet points):

> **The Honorable Richard J. Walker,** Court of Common Pleas of Allegheny County, Civil

Division, Pittsburgh, PA
Legal Intern, December 2008
Observed court proceedings in local trial court. Assisted judicial clerks with administrative tasks. Attended hearings and trials, including a contract dispute. Learned basic legal research methods. Helped proofread opinions and memoranda.

The Honorable Richard J. Walker, Court of Common Pleas of Allegheny County, Civil Division, Pittsburgh, PA
Legal Intern, December 2008

- Observed court proceedings in local trial court
- Assisted judicial clerks with administrative tasks
- Attended hearings and trials, including a contract dispute
- Learned basic legal research methods
- Helped proofread opinions and memoranda

Memorandums or Memoranda?

In "Let's Call the Whole Thing Off," Fred Astaire sang, "you like to-may-to and I like to-mah-to…." Some words and phrases are definitely a matter of opinion. For example, "memorandum" is the singular form of the noun. Yet you will see two alternative plural versions of that word: memoranda and memorandums. Which is correct? If you've studied Latin, the plural form of memorandum is memoranda. An acceptable alternative version is memorandums. Decide and be consistent. I follow my high school Latin teacher and go with memoranda.

In choosing between American English spelling and British English spellings, use American English spelling. Don't let your computer's spell check program steer you wrong. For instance:

American English	British English
Judgment	Judgement
License	Licence
Argument	Arguement
Defense	Defence
Honor	Honour
Color	Colour
Fulfill	Fulfil
Theater	Theatre
Center	Centre

If the title of your employer or a location is spelled a particular way, then—of course—go with the conventional spelling as noted.

Action Verbs

Enliven your law school résumé and describe your experience more fully using these action verbs:

Achieved	Counseled
Advised	Drafted
Analyzed	Evaluated
Assessed	Formulated
Communicated	Gathered
Compiled	Interpreted
Composed	Investigated

Led	Resolved
Negotiated	Responded
Organized	Reviewed
Oversaw	Solved
Planned	Studied
Prepared	Summarized
Presented	Supervised
Provided	Wrote
Researched	

Other

The final section of a law school résumé is the amorphous "Other" section, also called "Additional Information," "Other Skills" or "Personal." This is a final catch-all section where you can dazzle an employer with some cool tidbits about yourself. Some law school career services offices require that law students list an "Other" section; for most law schools this information is purely optional.

Generally, the other section is a place to describe skills, achievements or interests such as:

- Foreign languages (either fluency or proficiency)
- Interesting travel outside the U.S.
- Remarkable or unusual hobbies or sports
- Professional licenses (real estate, brokerage, insurance, financial planning or advising)

Some examples of interesting "Other" activities that merit inclusion:

- Training for half-marathon

- Completed the 2008 Marine Corps Marathon
- Licensed professional pilot
- Climbed Mt. Ranier
- Glassblowing
- Appearances in community theater productions

Do not list mundane things that many people enjoy doing: reading, going to movies, lifting weights, walking, or traveling. Entries like these do not add to an understanding of who you are. If that's the extent of your "Other" interests, just skip this section. You will not be penalized for focusing attention on your credentials.

Also, be wary of puffing your credentials. Don't say that you're fluent in a language unless you're truly fluent. Similarly, don't say that you enjoy fencing when you took a non-credit course during your freshman year in college and haven't touched an epee in years. Be scrupulously truthful and avoid embarrassment during an interview.

Page length for law résumés

Here's the general rule: One page for every decade of work experience you list.

1 résumé page = 10 years' work experience

If you are fresh out of college or took a year off before starting law school, your résumé ought to be one page. Unless you have done something truly extraordinary or had multiple jobs that are relevant to a legal employer, limit yourself to one page.

The one-page rule is a general rule. There are exceptions and you should not feel that you must comply, but keep in mind that employers spend only a few seconds scanning a résumé. You'd better have material that's worth turning the page for—and it better not be the fact that you were a Pre-School Teacher's Aide during your freshman year of college.

If your résumé runs longer than one page, be sure to number your pages so an employer clearly sees that there is more than one page. Sometimes pages get lost or misplaced at law offices and you want to insure that a potential employer sees all of your experiences, not just page one.

Do not include on your law school résumé

The following information should not appear on your résumé because it is either irrelevant to an employer's decision-making process or provides information that could be used in a discriminatory manner (whether intentionally or unintentionally). While you may see this information listed on business school résumés or other professional résumés, the following personal information does not appear on a law school résumé.

- **Social security number.** Aside from identity theft concerns, do not disclose your social security number in a résumé. Many employers will need this information later to do a security check or to issue a paycheck, but this information does not appear on your résumé.

- **LSAT Score.** Your LSAT score is irrelevant to your hiring prospects and is of no value to an employer. After all, the LSAT is a test of aptitude, not performance. Therefore, once you are accepted to law school, the relevant information about performance can be measured by your grades and class rank.

- **Age**. Not only irrelevant, but potentially discriminatory information to provide if you are over age 40.

- **References**. The throw-away line that appears at the bottom of so many résumés states "references available upon request." You should keep a separate list of references (name, title, phone, e-mail) to offer to employers, but the line at the bottom of your résumé is just taking up space.

- **Health.** This listing seems common on business résumés and yet wholly irrelevant and potentially discriminatory to boot. Have you ever seen a résumé that lists "Health: Not so great"? No. Everyone says "Health: Excellent". Do not include this.

- **Marital Status.** Irrelevant and potentially discriminatory information, as is information about children.

- **Photo.** Irrelevant and possibly contrary to employment discrimination laws.

- **U.S. Citizenship.** Generally irrelevant. Exception: Post-9/11, many federal and some state agencies now require proof of citizenship for employment, even for summer employment. If you are foreign-born and want to signal to an employer that you are eligible for employment, list your immigration status at the bottom of your résumé or in the body of your cover letter.

Carefully consider before including on your résumé

While the following items don't fall into the "do not list" category, think carefully before including the following information on your résumé:

- Political affiliation
- Religious affiliation
- Sexual orientation
- Specific partisan causes

Employers—flawed human beings that they are—will draw conclusions about you based on your résumé before meeting you in person. Therefore, if you provide information that may be deemed controversial, partisan, or indicative of a certain religious or political persuasion, you may knock yourself out of the running before you even get to the interview stage.

There is a debate—"to list or not to list"—and you should decide the best course of action for you. On one side of the debate are the individuals who say, "I've gotta be me ... a potential employer needs to know up front that I am a staunch Republican." That's fine. But keep in mind that, despite strong academic credentials, you may take yourself out of contention for a job because the person opening the envelope sees that you are a member of the College Republicans and decides he or she just doesn't want to meet you. He may be a staunch Democrat. She may have been married to a Republican once and now hates all Republicans. Before you shout, "but that's discrimination!", remember that you will never know if it was simply a very competitive job market, a candidate with better credentials, or your political affiliation that knocked you out of the running.

The flip side of the debate goes like this: "Better to list general information that strongly correlates to academic achievement, work experience, and other indicators of future success. Get the interview and meet the people for whom I will be working. When we meet each other, I can decide at that time—or later—to share my political views, religious affiliation, or sexual orientation. My goal right now is to find a job."

There is no right answer here. Here are some suggestions for coming to a conclusion:

Political affiliation. College Republicans, Young Democrats, Communist Party, Green Party. Listing one's political affiliation can cut both ways. If you have a serious inclination toward a particular party and feel this information is both relevant and essential to your candidacy, then list this information. For instance, if you want to be hired as a summer intern with the Democratic National Committee or with the conservative American Enterprise Institute, then listing your political bona fides can be deemed relevant. For a private law firm, judicial clerkship or government agency, however, your political affiliation will likely be less helpful in most instances.

Religious affiliation. If your religious affiliation is essential to your identity and if you have had particular work or travel experiences related to your faith, then list this information. Keep in mind, however, that some employers will relate to your experiences and others will not. For instance, if you want to work as an intern for the Catholic League for Religious and Civil Rights, then listing that you graduated from a Catholic high school, served on a Church-sponsored mission to South America, or are an active member of the Newman Society, would be relevant.

Sexual orientation. Should you list that you are a member of the Lesbian, Gay, Bisexual and Transgendered Law Student Association? This is a difficult issue and students need to follow their conscience about providing this information on their résumés. Listing this information "outs" you to an employer. Do you want to furnish this information now, later, or never? Your call.

Specific partisan causes. Do you support reproductive choice? Are you a vegan who is anti-fur? If you are cause-oriented person and this information is relevant to your employment history and to future employers, then list this information. For instance, if you are seeking employment this summer with People for the Ethical Treatment of Animals (PETA), then you ought to list all related human rights and animal rights organizations to which you belong and have a leadership role.

Tip: Ask a staff professional in your career services office to review your résumé before you engage in a job search so there's no doubt that your document is professional, showcases your experience appropriately, and is formatted clearly.

Q. I need help writing a cover letter! What should I emphasize? Do employers bother to read cover letters or do they refer to the résumés first?

A. Do not be mistaken: Employers read cover letters carefully. Very carefully. Your cover letter is the most important advocacy tool in your job search process because it speaks for you in your absence. It tells an employer, "hire me: here's why."

Your cover letter also serves as your writing sample. Employers realize that a cover letter is, perhaps, the most accurate rendering of your writing style and tone. Everyone knows that a writing sample is heavily edited by others and by the time it is presented to an employer, it may not represent your original writing style, grammar, syntax or tone.

Therefore, take your cover letter seriously. This is your chance to communicate your interest, skills and motivation to an employer. Drafting an effective cover letter may take some time and effort, but the result will be a well-considered, thoughtful communiqué to a potential employer.

Cover Letter Tips

- **Create a model cover letter and then tailor it for particular employers.** You need not re-invent the wheel every time you write to an employer. That would be exhausting and time-consuming. However, if you can draft some model paragraphs, then you can save time and customize a letter to target a particular employer or practice area.

- **Don't regurgitate your résumé.** Many law students mistakenly assume that if they simply recite every entry on their résumé, they will have written a good cover letter. This is, simply stated, a lazy and ineffective approach to cover letter writing. Your résumé is included along with your cover letter. Why waste the paper simply reciting what's already there? This is your opportunity to highlight the important experiences, the formative experiences, or information that is not listed on your résumé.

- **Keep it short and to-the-point.** Generally, a cover letter ought to be three or four short paragraphs that concisely describe your interest and motivation for applying to a particular employer. Ask yourself: "Why am I writing to this particular employer? What is my motivation for working here?" If your answer to these questions is: "Who really cares? I just want a job!" then it's time to take a break, explore your priorities, and sit down to write when you are properly motivated and enthused. Employers see through the "I just want a job!" letters in an nanosecond. The student who can convey genuine interest, enthusiasm, and care—regardless of one's grades—will be at an advantage. Therefore, take time to ask yourself these questions:

- Why am I writing to this particular employer?
- What is my motivation for working here?
- What distinguishes me from other candidates?

If you can successfully answer these questions through your cover letter, then you will truly be serving as an advocate for yourself.

A Paragraph-by-Paragraph Guide to Your Cover Letter

Paragraph 1: This is the "hello-here's-who-I-am-and-what-I-want" paragraph. Directly and concisely explain why you are writing and what you want. This is also the place to describe any connections you might have to the addressee. Don't bury valuable information in the body of the cover letter, place it front and center. For example:

"I am second-year law student at _____ and I am seeking a summer position with the Marvel County District Attorneys' Office."

If you are responding to a job posting, consider this introductory sentence:

"I am writing in response to your job posting for a law clerk through The Harcourt County Bar Reporter. As a second-year law student with a strong interest in family law, I have a demonstrated interest in legal research and writing for a trial court judge."

If you need to name-drop a networking connection (always helpful), then consider this:

"Professor Alvin Smith recommended that I contact you because of your expertise in the area of tax law. I am a second-year student at _____ with a strong interest in tax law."

Paragraph 2: This is the skills and motivation section of your cover letter. This information can be set forth in one paragraph or possibly two. It's purely a judgment call based upon how much you have to say and what seems appropriate. Do not feel constrained to explain everything in on paragraph if it doesn't work for you. Otherwise, you'll end up with a fifteen-line paragraph and that doesn't look right.

The middle section represents the heart of your cover letter. This should not be a recitation of your résumé. Rather, this ought to describe specific experiences, skills and your modus operandi for writing. This may be the hardest paragraph to write, but it's the most telling. A mass mailing letter throws a lot of information in no particular order and hopes for the best. A well-written, thoughtful cover letter writer takes a step back and asks:

- What would this particular employer (or type of employer) want to know about me, either from my résumé or that may not be readily apparent from my résumé?

- What is motivating me to contact this employer?

- What specific skills do I bring to bear that would directly interest this particular employer or type of employer?

- Why do you want to work in this city or town? (Note: When applying for jobs in smaller markets or rural areas, try—whenever possible—to explain your connection to or interest in the area. It's not necessary to explain why you want to live in San Francisco, Chicago, Washington, D.C., New York City, or other large metropolitan areas. However, think about drawing connections when you are looking in smaller markets or rural areas and your résumé does not clearly indicate your connection to that area.

You may read this and say to yourself, "here's what's motivating me: I need a job, any job." Stop and reconsider if just any job will do. The underlying attitude that you "need a job, any job" will, no doubt, be conveyed in a lackluster cover letter. Take a moment and really examine what is motivating you and help connect you to a potential employer. Employers can gain a strong sense from a cover letter if the writer truly cares and is engaged in the desire to find a good fit for themselves, or if they are—literally—just mailing it in.

If you really want to make your cover letter shine with enthusiasm and sincere interest, then consider the following:

"My interest in family law stems from my desire to help families and individuals thrive despite difficult times. My family course with Professor Smith gave me a passion for helping solve marital disputes fairly and to learn the complexities of foreign adoption procedures."

"My desire to become a federal public defender began when I was in college. I took a course on 'The Death Penalty and Society' and became enthralled with the integral role that public defenders play in assuring that justice prevails. After that experience, I spent my senior year researching and writing an honors thesis on capital punishment laws worldwide."

"As a Columbus, Ohio native, I am committed to returning home after graduation to develop a successful general litigation practice. I am seeking a summer job with a small law firm in Columbus this summer in anticipation of returning home after I graduate next year."

Tell an employer what makes you unique. Have you overcome hurdles? What distinguishes you from the competition? What is motivating you to apply to this particular firm? Why are you interested in this city or town? These are all relevant and important questions for you to address.

Do not waste space with self-serving statements. For example: "I am hard-working, diligent, and committed to excellence"—who isn't? Give the reader the facts to back up your statements. This is not perceived as bragging, but rather an important time to advocate on your behalf. This is particularly important and relevant if your grades are not outstanding. For example:

"I graduated from _____ with high honors while working two part-time jobs in order to defray the cost of my education. This experience taught me the importance of hard work, dedication, and sacrifice. These are skills that I bring to you as a summer law clerk."

"Despite the challenges of life as an NCAA scholar-athlete, I balanced a rigorous tennis competition schedule with a full load of courses in the history department. As a result of focus and hard work, I graduated with honors in my major and distinguished myself as the 2007 Student Athlete of the Year."

"After college, I chose to work as a paralegal at a large New York law firm in order to understand better the demands of the legal profession. Having experienced those challenges, I know that a smaller firm would complement my desire to have client contact earlier in my career and work in the courtroom with more frequency."

One final note: Avoid those ridiculously self-serving and empty statements such as "I was attracted to your firm because of its excellent reputation." Oh? Are you really in a position to determine a firm's reputation? Is a firm's listing in Martindale-Hubbell grounds for an excellent reputation? Who knows? Bottom line: it's self-serving and fawning to write these sentiments and employers view these as fluff and the stuff of mass mailings.

Paragraph 3 (the closing paragraph): This is your "thanks-I-look-forward-to-hearing-from-you" closing. It's fairly simple and straightforward:

"Thank you for your consideration. I would be pleased to speak with you further about my credentials. I can be reached at _____."

The closing paragraph is also a good opportunity to open the door for the next step. This is particularly helpful for smaller employers that cannot afford to fly you in for an interview. Make life easy and give the employer an opportunity to pick up the phone and call you. For example:

"Thank you for your consideration. I would be pleased to discuss my credentials with you in person. I will be visiting my family in Columbus during Thanksgiving vacation and would be available to interview at your convenience."

Any of the following closing words are appropriate for a cover letter:

> Sincerely,
> Yours truly,
> Sincerely yours,
> Very truly yours,

I'm a fan of the simple but straightforward "sincerely"—after all, if you can't be sincere with your cover letter, what can you be sincere about in this world?

Bottom line: Write with sincerity and do not be afraid to demonstrate your motivations and accomplishments to a potential employer. Merely reciting your résumé credentials will not distinguish you and may, in fact, demonstrate your lack of desire to find a job.

Q. I maintain a Facebook page to stay in touch with friends. I have photos from vacations, parties, and celebrations. Should I remove this information?

A. Your Internet image can impact your ability to be hired. More and more employers—whether law firms, government agencies, or non-legal employers—are taking a look at your presence on the Internet. While statistics for legal employers are not available, anecdotal evidence abounds that employers (or the associates taking you to lunch) will Google your name and see what comes up.

Keep a squeaky clean Internet presence to avoid any problems. This means removing all photos of you holding liquor, cigarettes, literally any "smoking gun" that could cause an employer to question your judgment. Clean up your personal web site, social networking site, YouTube, or anywhere else where your name or image may come up in a non-professional context. You may decide to suspend your Facebook, MySpace, or other pages while you job search.

While it's probably true that the partners you meet today may have, in their murky past, also taken tasteless party photos holding liquor bottles, the fact is that they didn't have the technology to post their youthful indiscretions for the whole world to see. The Internet generation may not have the exclusive license on stupidity and poor taste, but you now have the ability to broadcast it to the entire universe.

If you have a serious image issue (including misappropriation of your identity, inappropriate comments taken out of context, or inappropriate images), talk to your career services office for advice. You may want to hire a web de-optimization service, such as ReputationDefender.com, to help you conduct some Internet damage control.

Also be prepared to discuss questionable Internet material at your interview to head off trouble from the get-go.

Internet Image Tips for Law Students

Assume that employers will conduct electronic background checks on you.

- Perform a regular online search of your name (Google, Yahoo, Ask) to determine what information comes up. If necessary, consider hiring a service to help polish your online image and de-optimize harmful material.

- Set all online profiles to "private", letting in only those you trust and know personally. Also check your friends' profiles on a regular basis to monitor the types of pictures and comments being posted about you. Tell your friends to respect your desire not to be commented upon or to have photos posted at this time.

> - If you blog or post comments on message boards, do so with extreme caution. Excessive blogging, particularly about work or your personal life, may be viewed critically by legal employers who value discretion and good judgment.
>
> - Personal web pages can be effective ways to market yourself beyond a traditional résumé; however, content must remain professional at all times. Avoid links to other sites that may demonstrate poor judgment.

Netiquette Tips
Telephone

- Record a professional voicemail message on both your home phone and your cell phone. No singing, rhyming, edgy, or funny messages. No music or distracting noise in the background. Record your message in a quiet space.

  Here is a sample message that is professional: "Hello, you have reached the voicemail of (your name here). I am not available to take your call right now. Please leave your name, telephone number and a brief message and I will return your call as soon as possible."

- Return phone calls within the same business day, if possible. Most lawyers will tell you that responding to voicemail messages within four hours is optimal, so follow suit.

- Choose a professional-sounding ring tone for your cell phone.

- Use your good judgment when deciding when to keep your cell phone on, when to place it on vibrate, and when to turn it off completely.

- Check your voicemail messages on a regular basis, at least twice a day, in the morning and in the evening.

E-mail

- When composing e-mail messages (whether on computer or Black-Berry), write as though you were drafting professional correspondence. Use correct grammar and punctuation at all times. No slang or "IM" lingo.

- When composing e-mail messages, keep in mind that these writings are discoverable during litigation. Therefore, use good judgment regarding content. Opposing counsel may be reading your clever observations about misconduct, culpability, ethical violations, and other high crimes and misdemeanors.

- Assume that everything will be forwarded (and if you tell someone the content is confidential or "for your eyes only"). Therefore, use caution when responding to e-mails.

- Before you hit "send," make sure that you are sending the e-mail to the correct recipient. If you're tired or not paying attention, that e-mail you wanted to send to your girlfriend Alison might, instead, be going to "All Recipients" on your law firm's distribution list. Don't laugh, it's happened.

- Keep your e-mail address completely professional. For example, do not use suggestive names that hint at poor judgment such as hotmama@aol.com or singlesexylwyer@gmail.com. Keep it factual: first name, last name or some combination thereof and you avoid problems.

- Use your work computer solely for professional purposes. Do not subscribe to non-professional list-serv lists, shop online, or play games.

- Check your e-mail on a regular basis and respond promptly. You do not have to respond right away, but it is always helpful to the sender to write, "I have received your e-mail and will respond shortly." Nothing can irk a sender more than an unacknowledged e-mail. For instance, if you are in court and know that you cannot communicate right away, either send a message explaining your situation or ask your secretary to make contact. Establish a time to respond more properly and thoughtfully. Then keep your promise by noting that you need to address an outstanding issue.

BlackBerry, Bluetooth headsets and other electronic devices

- Do not wear your Bluetooth accessory to meetings or meals. Simply stated, it's rude. If communicating with someone is that urgent, excuse yourself from the table or meeting and communicate privately. To define "urgent" specifically, I mean waiting for an organ transplant for yourself or a loved one, waiting to hear about a family member in labor, and so forth.

- Do not text during meetings or meals. If communication is that urgent, excuse yourself from the table or meeting and communicate privately. It is disrespectful to text messages when in the company of another either in a social setting or during a meeting. Respect others' time by being attentive or excuse yourself from the action and attend to business.

- Do not wear your iPod while working; leave it at home or save it for personal time such as the commute to and from work. You may love listening to music while you cite-check but when a partner stands in your doorway, you should acknowledge her presence immediately.

Creating Parameters for BlackBerry Users

Possessing a BlackBerry does not mean that you must be accessible 24/7. Learning to create parameters is an important part of your development not only as a lawyer but your general level of happiness as a person. BlackBerries (and cell phones) can be wonderful communication devices but they can also run your life if you let them.

Try to avoid developing what I like to call "BlackBerry Addictive Disorder" (BAD). No pun intended, many BlackBerry users find themselves in truly bad situations by being accessible to bosses and clients 24/7. Fortunately, you can manage your Blackberry accessibility while remaining productive. For starters, define what would be a reasonable period within which to respond to an e-mail. Two hours? One hour? Only 30 minutes? Whatever your chosen interval, try turning your BlackBerry off for that period; when you turn it back on, respond immediately to whatever shows up that demands your attention. This will enable you to focus on deadlines, research, and other important work-related tasks without interruption.

In addition, try turning off the "buzzing" notification, so that an incoming message does not immediately divert your attention; then check your BlackBerry only when you feel the need, not when the technology forces you to react. In time, you will grow comfortable checking once an hour or so, and enjoy the relatively quiet calm of the in-between times to complete projects, return phone calls, and stay focused on the task at hand.

What does the National Association for Law Placement (NALP) have to say about the Internet and the recruiting process? The following is taken from the Interpretation of NALP Principles and Standards available online at www.nalp.org:

Q. What are the responsibilities of employers, candidates and law schools regarding the use of information on the Internet during the recruiting process?

A. Employers should use valid, job related criteria when evaluating candidates. Information learned about candidates on the Internet that has no predictive value with respect to employment performance, should not be relied upon by employers in the hiring process. If an employer obtains information on the Internet about a candidate that may have predictive value with respect to employment performance, the employer should make good faith efforts to determine the accuracy and reliability of the source of such information prior to using that information in evaluating the candidate.

Candidates should learn as much as possible about target employers and the nature of their positions. When conducting research into employers on the Internet, candidates should make good faith efforts to determine the accuracy and reliability of the source of the information they obtain prior to using that information in evaluating the employer.

Law schools should counsel students about the importance of maintaining a professional image on the Internet; the propriety of providing information on the Internet about fellow candidates and employers; and the importance of making good faith efforts to determine the accuracy and reliability of the source of information they obtain about employers on the Internet during the recruiting process.

–NALP Principles & Standards, Part II.C.1; Part III.A.2; and Part IV.E.3

For further reading on Internet issues, including e-mail and other electronic communication see:

Send: The Essential Guide to Email for Office and Home by David Shipley and Will Schwalbe (Knopf, 2007). This concise and wonderfully written guide explains the details so that you can navigate office and personal email successfully.

The Modern Rules of Business Etiquette by Donna Gerson and David Gerson (2008). Published by American Bar Association Publishing, this book is specifically written for law students and lawyers.

Q. What is networking? How important is networking to finding a job this summer?

A. "Networking is the process by which an individual gathers information and, in turn, shares information with others, creating and enhancing connections for mutual benefit."

Why is Networking Important?

The personal connections created through networking can offer the most powerful tools for you to find a job this summer, particularly when seeking jobs with small firms and public interest organizations. The personal touch cannot be overstated in legal job searching. While on-campus interviewing encourages a "point-and-click" mentality toward the job search, the reality of most job-hunting involves impersonal connections.

"If there's only one thing second-year students should do to ensure a successful job search, it's networking," notes Carole Montgomery, Director of the Career Development Office at The George Washington University Law School. "Networking includes attendance at law firm receptions, educational programs featuring practitioners offered throughout the academic year, and self-initiated meetings such as informational interviews. Law students need to see what it's really like to work at a particular firm. If you attend receptions and educational programs, you can talk one-on-one with attorneys and really learn. As a result, you will be able to make more knowledgeable choices. Because our law school uses a bidding system for OCI (you can only apply to so many employers through OCI), law students need to make intelligent choices about the best 'fit' going forward .... You can't apply to every single firm, so make smart choices by networking."

Why Do You Avoid Networking?

Law students avoid networking for many reasons, including:

- "It's distasteful." The idea of developing a relationship in order to ask for something runs counter to many people's feelings of good taste and appropriateness.

- "Asking for help shows weakness." Why make yourself vulnerable to a successful professional by showing that you don't know who to ask, what to do, or that you lack knowledge?

- "I can't stand the thought of being rejected." Some students cower at the idea of asking for help and then not receiving help. To avoid being rejected or not receiving a prompt response from an email inquiry or phone call, some law students would rather not make the effort at all.

- "I don't have time." Who has time to research networking contacts, send inquiries, arrange meetings, and then follow up?

- "I'm shy." Many law students assume that networking is only about glad-handing at parties.

- "Bragging about your achievements is rude—that's what networking is all about." Law students assume that you have to crow about your achievements to get attention.

- "I don't know how to network." Students lack the knowledge, skills, encouragement, and experience to network effectively.

Let's dispel some myths:
- Networking is about connecting with others, not about asking for a job.

- Most jobs are filled through either personal connections or personal recommendations from individuals who can vouch for you. It makes sense, therefore, to be present in both your law school community and your legal community. Your good name can make a tremendous difference in whether you get the nod for a job or not.

- You don't need to be a social butterfly to be a successful connector. In truth, you need to be a good listener.

- You must make time to cultivate professional connections.

Networking is important for students in the top half of the class

Whether you're at the top of your class or the very bottom, connecting with practitioners ought to be a top priority throughout law school. Even if you find a summer associate job through the OCI process and succeed in receiving a full-time offer, focus on building your network while in law school. Why? Your next job search will not involve the "point-and-click" simplicity of OCI. When the time comes to move on to your next job, who are you going to contact? Are you going to respond to an ad in your bar newspaper? Possibly. Will you seek the assistance of a headhunter? Possibly. Nonetheless, nothing can substitute for having a network of colleagues, peers and more senior attorneys, who know you, like you, and understand what you're seeking. That kind of network can trump any public posting or fee-for-hire service. "Networking enables you to build relationships for the next position you seek," observes Carole Montgomery of The George Washington University Law School. "Building these connections will be very important after law school."

Networking is essential if you're at the bottom of your class

"For law students who are toward the bottom of the class, networking is everything," observes George Washington's Carole Montgomery. "You need to capture the attention of employers with other credentials besides grades. Therefore, the personal connections are especially important."

Travel Outside Your "Comfort Zone"

A law student at a D.C. area law school wanted to practice in sports and entertainment law. He visited his career services office where he learned the ins and outs of practice and the highly competitive nature of these jobs. The career services advisor told the law student that the Virginia Bar Association was holding a sports and entertainment law program featuring successful practitioners at the University of Virginia School of Law. He was advised to call and inquire about a price break for law students (which he received) and then took the time to drive to Charlottesville to meet and network with sports and entertainment law professionals. The reward: a fistful of business cards and contacts.

On the Importance of Being Nice, Because You Never Know!

Matthew L. Pascocello of the Office of Career & Professional Development at American University Washington College of Law shares this important anecdote:

"A third-year student with strong credentials was still seeking a job in April before graduation. Has had had numerous interviews and callbacks, but zero offers throughout OCI. A meeting with the student earlier in the semester revealed that he had a very inflated ego and an arrogant attitude that you should have to work to win him over, instead of vice versa.

"Apparently, this attitude had served him just fine in life... until now. My meeting with the student, which was brutally honest, included a stern discussion about how obnoxiously he presented himself and how this was certainly a turn-off to potential employers. We hashed out a targeted networking approach to New York City firms and we rehearsed how he should approach and conduct himself during informational interviews. To his credit, he really took my comments to heart and worked to adjust his attitude and approach.

"Fast-forward a month later when he visited my office elated that he just landed a full-time job with a boutique firm in New York! The day before he was to meet with a name partner in the law firm for an informational interview, he happened to be working out at the university gym on campus. During his workout, an undergraduate student struck up a conversation with him based on a particular T-shirt the law student was wearing. According to the law student, he ordinarily would have ignored the kid, but he remembered the conversation we had and decided to be nice and actually converse with the undergraduate, instead.

"The next day during his informational interview with the name partner at the law firm, the partner turns to him and said, with a smile on his face, 'I heard you were really nice to my son yesterday at the campus gym. I really appreciate that.'

"Guess where he got the offer?"

Easy Networking Tips

· Make a real commitment to connect with lawyers, law professors, and others to learn about the profession. Don't assume that you can get all the information you need from books and articles. Get out and meet people who are doing the kind of work you think you want to do!

· Start inside your law school: attend educational programs offered by your career services office, student groups, and faculty. Your law school offers a wide range of free, informal learning experiences with top professionals. What do you have to lose? Many law school programs will lure students with free food. Grab a slice of pizza and hear what others have to say.

· Use your law school and college alumni mentor network to make connections. Don't be shy! Not every connection will be a "home run." Some people may ignore you, others may not be available right away due to busy schedules. So what? You put yourself at an advantage by meeting others and learning first-hand.

· Join a bar association as a law student. Many bar associations now offer very affordable law student memberships. Join, but don't just put the membership on your résumé.

Attend a continuing legal education (CLE) class in a subject matter that interests you. Participate on a committee, such as the Young Lawyers' Division, and otherwise become involved in some level.

· Have a list of questions that you can ask a networking contact.

· Always follow up and keep the connection alive.

Read More

The following books can help you learn more about networking skills and strategies:

Be Your Own Mentor: Strategies from Top Women on the Secrets of Success by Sheila Wellington and Betty Spense (Random House, 2001). Chapter 6 deals with networking and contains very good information.

Building Career Connections: Networking Tools for Law Students and New Lawyers by Donna Gerson (NALP, 2007).

The Art of Friendship: 70 Simple Rules for Making Meaningful Connections by Roger Horchow and Sally Horchow (Quick Packaging, 2005).

What Do I Say Next? Talking Your Way to Business and Social Success by Susan RoAne (Grand Central Publishing, 1997).

How to Work a Room, Revised Edition: Your Essential Guide to Savvy Socializing by Susan RoAne (Collins Living, 2007).

The Secrets of Savvy Networking: How to Make the Best Connections for Business and Personal Success by Susan RoAne (Grand Central Publishing, 1993).

Networking: Insiders' Strategies for Tapping the Hidden Market Where Most Jobs Are Found by Douglas B. Richardson (John Wiley & Sons, Inc., 1994).

Savvy Networking: 118 Fast & Effective Tips for Business Success by Andrea Nierenberg (Capital Books, 2007).

Never Eat Alone: And Other Secrets to Success, One Relationship at a Time by Keith Ferrazzi and Tahl Raz (Doubleday Busines, 2005).

Targeting the Job You Want by Kate Wendleton (3rd ed., Delmar Cengage Learning, 2000). This book is produced by the Five O'Clock Club, a networking and career counseling organization.

The Networking Survival Guide: Get the Success You Want By Tapping Into the People You Know by Diane Darling (McGraw Hill, 2003).

Q. What is informational inter-viewing? Why is it important to my professional development?

A. It's not just what you know, it's who you know. Informational interviewing en-ables you to learn first-hand about career paths, ask questions, and receive honest feedback from individuals who have objec-tive experience. Many students shy away from contacting lawyers—whether in tradi-tional or non-traditional fields—for many reasons: they are shy, they don't want to appear unknowledgeable, they don't want to bother a busy professional, or they feel that they're intruding. Don't fall prey to these sorts of thoughts. If you don't ask the experts—those doing the kind of work you think you want to pursue—how can you ever learn?

Most law schools offer alumni mentoring networks of one sort or another. Ask for details at your career services office. These networks are composed of graduates who have requested that they be listed and contacted by law students; thus, they're a friendly source of career information.

Write to individuals via e-mail or regular mail and request the opportunity to meet and speak in person. If you are conducting a long-distance search and your contact is in a distant location, then schedule time to speak on the phone. Many mentor re-lationships can be initiated by phone and then continued by an in-person meeting.

What do you say when requesting an in-formational interview? It's pretty straightforward: Introduce yourself, explain your situation and politely ask for some time to ask questions and learn more. Here's an example of an e-mail request:

> Dear Ms. Smith,
> The Law School Alumni Network provided your name as a contact for law students interested in health care law. I am a second-year law students with a strong interest in pursuing a career in hospital law. I am currently taking "Health Law Basics" with Professor Jones and am enrolled in the Health Law Clinic in the spring semester. In addition to my academic courses, I am anxious to speak with a practitioner about career paths in the St. Louis area. If you would be willing to meet with me at your convenience, I would be grateful for the opportunity to ask you questions about health law. Please let me know if you would like to see a copy of my résumé; I am always interested in receiving feedback about how I present my credentials. Thank you in advance for considering my request. The Law School Alumni Network is a wonderful resource for law students and I appreciate your time.
>
> Sincerely,
> Jane Student
> jstudent@lawschool.edu
> Phone number

Informational Interview Checklist

- Find out if your law school offers an alumni mentor network (a listing of graduates who are willing to be contacted for career advice);

- Find out if your college offers an alumni mentor network. It's perfectly acceptable to tap into your undergraduate network to find help;

- If you cannot find a good match through either your college or law school, then conduct independent research using Martindale-Hubbell to find lawyers who are practicing in your area of interest and/or area of the country;

- Contact individuals by e-mail (if e-mail addresses are provided). E-mail is the easiest way to initiate contact because it does not force the recipient to respond right away. E-mail also enables the recipient to forward your e-mail to colleagues and friends. A phone call—while perfectly appropriate—can interrupt a busy professional and force them to respond to you directly. You never know what types of deadlines or crises are going on in a person's life. E-mail is the kindest method of communication, second only to a typewritten letter.

- Schedule a brief meeting, either at the person's office or a coffee shop. Assume that you are paying for the person's coffee unless they offer to take you out (which is always a kind gesture but not expected).

- Come prepared with a list of questions (see below).

- Never, ever ask for a job.

- Always ask for the names/contact information of other people to meet.

- Always say "thank you" both in person and in a subsequent correspondence.

- Always follow up with your progress and keep your network alive.

A career services professional shared this success story: "A very shy student visited the career services office. She wanted to work in higher education law but didn't know where to begin. The law student was given names of practitioners who practiced higher education law through our alumni mentor network and we encouraged her to reach out. Higher education law is a niche practice area and quite close-knit. While the law student was very reluctant to reach out (she hated the idea of cold-calling), she did make some calls to the alumni on the list. Three different practitioners invited her to lunch and, as a result, she forged connections, learned the ins and outs, and had a job search strategy that was realistic as a result."

Suggested Informational Interview Questions

The following questions can serve as springboards to broader conversations about practice areas, work/life balance, and other important issues for you to consider as you explore career options. Focus on questions that ask "why?" These types of questions typically evoke insightful answers.

- Why did you decide to practice in the area of _____?

- Why did you choose this particular firm/agency/non-profit organization for your career?

- Why did you choose to work in this particular city?

- Where do lawyers in your practice specialty tend to work? (private practice, government agency, public interest organization, NGO, etc.)

- Who are your clients and what types of cases or issues do you handle?

- What daily activities are you involved in your practice?

- What do you find rewarding about your practice area?

- How do people generally enter your field of practice?

- What skills do you think are most important to your practice area?

- What classes or law school experiences (for instance, externships, clinics,

> summer work experiences) do you
> recommend to students?
>
> · With whom do you suggest I speak
>   to learn more?

Informational Interview Etiquette

· Always follow up with a thank you within 24 hours of your meeting.

· Always keep records of your networking/informational interview contacts.

· Always calendar a follow-up message with specific information about the steps you have taken to learn more. It's particularly thoughtful to send a letter or e-mail when you secure a job to say "thank you again and let's keep in touch."

· Never ask for a job.

· Respect the confidentiality of your contact. Never name drop or use a contact's name without specific permission.

Q. How do I prepare for an interview? What types of questions can I expect to be asked?

A. An interview enables you to personally present your credentials and interests to a potential employer. In addition, an interview allows both parties—the interviewee and the interviewer—to determine that elusive hiring category, what is often called "fit."

Whether you are participating in On-Campus Interviewing (OCI) with large firms, interviewing with government agencies, or pursuing a job with a small law firm or public interest organization, the essentials rules of interviewing remain the same. Your job is to connect your skills and experience to the needs of the firm, while simultaneously emphasizing that you want to be working in this venue.

These tips will help you shine in interviews:

- Conduct research about the firm. Prior to your interview, conduct research so you know what practice areas the firm engages in, any recent publicity relating to cases or clients, and information about the lawyers with whom you will be interviewing. Always refer to the firm's web site as a starting point. Most firms, particularly large firms and government agencies, maintain web sites with information about principal practice areas, media

---

highlights, and lawyer profiles. Second, look the firm up on Martindale-Hubbell to see the firm profile and lawyer biographies. Finally, do a general Internet search (using Google, Ask or Yahoo) to see what recent stories may come up. In addition, ask a staff professional at your career services for any scoop they may have (for example, prominent alumni who work at the firm or agency). The more you know, the better.

- Prior research about the firm's location. This means, figure out in advance where the firm is located and have a fail-safe system to get you there on time. Anticipate rush hour traffic, road closings, parking lots snafus, and other unforeseen circumstances. Nothing puts the kibosh on an interview faster than arriving late and flustered.

- Understand the dress code and dress accordingly. Unless the firm says otherwise, dress in traditional interview attire. If you are told the firm is "business casual," dress accordingly but err on the side of being slightly overdressed rather than underdressed. As always, consult with your career services office to get the inside scoop and avoid needless stress.

- Anticipate objections to your candidacy. Are you worried about your grades? Concerned about your lack of experience? Stressed that you had a bad work experience last summer and don't want to talk about it with a potential employer? Relax! Nearly every law student has concerns about his or her credentials and experience. The issue here is to figure out which concerns are real and which concerns are trivial. How do you figure this out? Rather than guess, go to your career services office and talk to a staff professional about your concerns. Oftentimes, objections about grades or experience can be discussed and dealt with through rehearsal (see below). Rarely, a concern turns out to be a deal-breaker regarding an employer. Rather than stew about things you'd rather not discuss or are afraid to be asked by an interview, name your perceived objections and deal with them beforehand.

- Rehearse with a mock interview. A mock interview, arranged through your career services office, enables you to practice interview questions in a safe environment and rehearse answers to particularly difficult questions. Most law schools permit law students to schedule mock interviews and these can be videotaped. A mock interview helps you see how you really appear to an interviewer. For instance, are you clicking your pen or tapping your knees nervously during questions? Is your interview outfit inappropriate? Are you making appropriate eye contact? The video camera never lies. You can address externalities like verbal tics and physical nervousness head on. More importantly, when it comes to the content of your answers and finessing difficult questions, a mock interview enables you to practice advocating for yourself and taking the emotion out of the equation so you address employers' concerns head on.

- If you do not feel the need to schedule a mock interview, sit down by yourself or with friends and ask yourself the following questions:
  - Why did you decide to attend law school?
  - What did you decide to attend X law school?
  - Why do you want to work at this particular firm?
  - What skills or experiences do you bring that would make you a compelling candidate?
  - Why do you want to work in this city?
  - Where do you see yourself in five years?
  - Do you have any questions for me? (See below)

If you are interviewing at many firms and are not getting any call-back interviews or offers, it's a sign of trouble. You may think you're an exceptional interviewer, but you may be doing something profoundly wrong if you're not getting call-backs or offers. Before you lose out on too many opportunities, swallow your pride, walk into your career services office, and ask for help. It's typically the students who think they're great interviewers who are coming across as arrogant, unpleasant, or are approaching the process with misinformation. The faster you get help, the better.

Be ready with questions to ask the employer. Toward the conclusion of your interview, nearly every interviewer will ask you, "do you have any questions for me?" The only correct answer to this question is, "yes!" Even if you think you know everything about this particular firm, the only correct answer is "yes!" Even if every single interviewer at the firm asks you this very question as the individual interview session wraps up, you must answer "yes!" Unless you sincerely believe that the firm is not a good fit for your interests and credentials, then by all means say, "no, I have no questions for you." This will undoubtedly conclude the interview and your chances of receiving an offer. A "no" answer tells the interviewer that you are not interested in the firm, not motivated to learn more, and not desirous of receiving an offer. The question "do you have any questions for me?" is your chance to show your interest and research. Thus, it's not the juncture to ask something obvious; rather, now is your chance to learn more. Ask the interviewer about his or her own career path. For instance, you can ask motivational questions (the "why" questions) to get the interviewer to talk to you further:

- Why did you decide to practice at this firm?
- What distinguishes this firm from other firms?
- What are the advantages of working at a firm of this size versus a larger firm?
- Why did you decide to practice in this particular practice area?
- Do you enjoy your work?
- What do you enjoy about your work?
- What type of work do your summer law clerks engage in during the summer?
- I see you worked for a federal agency before going into private practice. Did you find that advantageous to your professional development?

When you ask questions of an employer, listen carefully and then—this is key—reflect back with a response that conveys your sincere interest. This is very important. Simply nodding your head in agreement does nothing to advocate for your candidacy. Instead, listen carefully and then answer with an affirmative statement that connects the interviewer's observations about the firm or her career path with your own. For instance:

> *Interviewee:* What distinguishes X,Y, Z firm from other labor law firms in St. Louis?

> *Interviewer:* X, Y, Z firm prides itself on its in-depth training program and its ability to find the finest minds committed to practicing management-side labor law. We've handled most of the high-profile cases in this federal district and advise some of the largest corporations in the state.

> *Interviewee:* That's great to hear because I'm very committed to practicing management-side labor law and have really worked to build my experience so I can hit the ground running. This past semester I took "Advanced Issues in Labor Law" with Professor White and this confirmed my commitment to practice at X, Y, Z firm.

Of course, this is not an invitation to simply nod in agreement and say anything to support your cause. And certainly do not try to offer contradictory information to different interviewers. The interviewers will either meet afterwards or complete evaluations and you do not want to appear at cross-purposes with different departments. Nonetheless, use the question-and-answer routine that concludes most interviews to state your case, advocate for yourself, and leave a lasting impression that you're enthusiastic and interested.

Remember: An interview ought to be a conversation, not an interrogation. Do not expect the interviewer to ask you questions and for you to respond accordingly. Engage in a conversation, show genuine interest, and connect your credentials to the firm's needs.

The Cheat Sheet—Questions about Woman-Friendly Employers

In September 2006, Flex-Time Lawyers LLC and the New York City Bar's Committee on Women in the Profession released "The Cheat Sheet," a list of suggested questions to help candidates select a woman-friendly employer (http://www.flextimelawyers.com/pdf/art3.pdf).

Dealing with Difficult Interviewers

You may meet with an especially contentious attorney who may challenge you, ask you pointed questions, or make you feel defensive. Do not get ruffled. Remain calm and stand your ground with the highest degree of civility. Being on the receiving end of cantankerous questioning is never easy, but law is not an easy profession and you will certainly encounter push-back throughout your career. Sometimes lawyers may be testing you to see your reaction. While I don't think it's necessarily fair to put law students in this position, if you do find yourself at the receiving end of a cantankerous exchange remember to disagree civilly and then try to redirect the conversation.

If you are dealing with truly improper questions or statements relating to gender, age, sexuality, religion, disability or nationality, you must raise this issue with your career services office directly.

Improper Questions to Ask Employers

Avoid asking questions relating to benefits, vacation, part-time, flex-time, billable hour minimums, perks, maternity/paternity policy, free lunches, summer associate social events, scheduling time for your honeymoon, and the like. Information relating to benefits is often available through the NALP Directory of Legal Employers. Furthermore, asking about these issues—and not substantive questions relating to education, client development, and career—will not reflect well on your seriousness as a professional.

Questions about Pro Bono Work

These days it's much more acceptable to ask about pro bono opportunities, although you do not want to monopolize the conversation with questions about pro bono work. You may come across as someone less interested in the business aspects of practice and more interest in a public interest career. Therefore, tread carefully when addressing these issues.

If you're interviewing in two cities: If questioned about other firms or locations where you are interviewing, be honest. It's perfectly fine to be considering other options. Simply have a good reason for seeking employment at this particular firm. If questioned about where else you may be interviewing, you are under no obligation to disclose this information although it can never hurt to let people know that others are considering you.

Completing the Interview

- **Show genuine interest.** You gain nothing by playing it cool or appearing aloof during interviews. Many students assume that appearing enthusiastic about receiving an offer will be viewed negatively. Nothing could be farther from the truth. Ask for the job and appear excited about the prospect of working for this employer (if you genuinely feel this is the case after the interview). You may want to close an interview by shaking hands with the interviewer and saying: "Thanks for the opportunity to speak with you. I really think this firm would be a great fit for my interests and goals. I would be delighted to work here." Yet another way to show interest is to come prepared with extra copies of résumés, writing samples, and reference letters in a portfolio or briefcase. Papers do sometimes get lost or misplaced at law firms and your ability to come prepared demonstrates genuine interest and professionalism.

- **Follow up.** After your interview, promptly send a thank you letter, preferably within 24 hours of your interview. The thank you letter need not be elaborate and you can keep a general template on file. I recommend a typed business correspondence, although it is becoming more and more acceptable to send e-mail (depending on the type of firm and the age of your interviewers). Certainly write to either the hiring partner or the recruiting manager to express your appreciation for their time. Name the individuals with whom you met and reiterate your strong interest in the firm. It's not necessary to write to every single person with whom you met, although you may feel moved to write to certain individuals separately. Thank you notes demonstrate sincere interest and can be counted in your favor. However, a poorly written or misspelled letter will be held against you. Other follow-up could involve a phone call or email while an offer is pending; however, you don't want to make a nuisance of yourself. At large firms, hiring committees meet at regular intervals during the on-campus interview season. If you're a very strong candidate, then you may receive an offer right away. If your credentials are good but not great, you may receive an offer but it may take a few weeks. If you are anxious about a possible offer, do not call to check in unless you have a good reason for doing so, such as a competing offer from another firm.

The Interview Lunch

In addition to interviews in the office, some employers—especially large firms—will often take a candidate out to either lunch, dinner or drinks. The purpose of a meal outside the office is to have the opportunity to speak more informally, observe you in a social setting, and show you some hospitality. Often, a summer associate candidate will be taken to lunch by junior associates who may be closer in age to you. The following are some guidelines to help you navigate the interview lunch:

- Even if you are being wined and dined, you are still in interview mode; do not let down your guard for one moment.

- Enjoy the camaraderie of being with people who are close in age to you, but always remember that you are being interviewed and they are not your friends. When the meal concludes, your dining partners will be completing evaluations of you.

- Remain professional at all times and keep the conversation on substantive issues and questions.

- Avoid consuming alcohol. If everyone is having an alcoholic beverage, then you may go with the flow and order one (but only one). Of course, if you do not drink alcohol for personal reasons, don't!

- Order "interview friendly" foods, items that can be easily cut with a fork and knife. Avoid messy foods and finger foods such as pastas, sandwiches, and foods requiring special equipment, such as lobster.

- Use impeccable table manners at all times. If you are nervous and need a refresher course, read *The Modern Rules of Business Etiquette* (ABA Publishing) which contains a section on table etiquette.

- Do not take food home from an interview meal. The purpose of the meal is to interview you further in a social setting, it's not to bring home leftovers to enjoy late at night.

Interview "No Show" Policies

Every law school has a policy relating to professionalism and interviews. Know your law school's policy and abide by the rules. In a nutshell, not showing up for an interview reflects poorly on both you and your law school. When interviewing with a firm, you must represent the highest level of professionalism.

Exploding Offers

What is an exploding offer? Essentially, it is an offer that self-destructs within a time frame and does not allow a law student to have the time, as dictated by the NALP Principles and Standards, to make a decision. For example, you have experienced an exploding offer when an employer makes you an offer (by letter, e-mail or phone) and says, "We have a limited number of summer associate slots and would really like to hire you. The first five candidates to accept our offer of employment will join our firm this summer...."

You may be saying, "huh?" Even though exploding offers are inherently unfair and arbitrary, occasionally a law firm will employ this method of making offers. Why? Some of it may be a simple lack of knowledge about acceptable hiring practices. For others it may be laziness on a grand scale. Instead of trying to choose who are the best candidates for the firm, ranking them and extending offers, the hiring partner will say to the staff professional, "just send a letter to everyone on our list and whoever replies first gets a job."

If this happens to you, immediately contact your career services office and let the director or dean handle this.

Interview Checklist

- Confirm the date, time and location of your interview
- Get directions
- If driving, figure out the parking situation
- Research the firm
- Rehearse either with a mock interview or on your own

- Arrive 5–10 minutes early
- Dress appropriately
- Have some questions prepared for your interviewer
- Be prepared to answer questions about every item on your résumé
- Know your writing sample backwards and forwards
- Treat everyone you meet with respect
- Bring extra copies of your résumé, writing sample, and list of references
- Greet interviewers with a firm handshake and a winning smile
- Make eye contact
- Keep the focus on your skills and experience
- Advocate for yourself, but do not act with arrogance
- Write a thank-you note promptly afterwards

To learn more:

"An Insider's Guide to Interviewing: Insights from the Employer's Perspective," a booklet published by the National Association for Law Placement (NALP) should be available from your career services office. It's full of good advice and tips!

Q. What is the best way to handle telephone interviews?

A. Telephone interviews are sometimes used to screen job candidates and narrow the pool of applicants who will be invited for second interviews in person. If you are interviewing with out-of-town employers, a telephone interview is a cost-effective way for an employer to talk with you initially. If your telephone interview goes well, you may be invited for a second interview. In some instances, employers will conduct the telephone interview and make you a job offer without a "call back" or second interview. You might expect this for first-summer jobs that are offered without compensation.

Impress a potential employer during a telephone interview with these tips:

- Be prepared. When you are actively engaged in the interview process, you ought to be prepared to interview on short notice. A lawyer, recruiting coordinator, or networking contact may call and ask if you have a few minutes to talk. Lawyers and hiring professionals can be tough to reach sometimes, so when someone calls you, be prepared to talk.

- Take the call in a quiet place where it's unlikely you will be interrupted. Turn off the radio, television, and mute the volume on your computer (an interviewer should not hear, "you've got mail!"). Clear the room of any live distractions, including kids and pets.

- Keep your résumé in front of you in clear view. Refer to it during the interview.

- Have a pen and paper for note taking.

- Avoid using a cell phone for a call (if an interview is scheduled in advance). Many career services offices now have private telephone rooms where you can schedule time to sit quietly and conduct a telephone interview. If that's not the case, then use your cell phone. Keep in mind, however, that it can be very frustrating to take a call on your cell phone and then lose the call because of poor reception.

- Do not smoke, chew gum, eat, or drink while interviewing on the telephone.

- Speak slowly and enunciate clearly. Take your time answering questions—this isn't a race!

- Write the word "SMILE" on a Post-It® note or piece of paper. Project a positive image and make sure the tone of your voice sounds confident and at ease.

- If it helps, stand up while you are speaking. For some people, standing helps you focus, keeps your circulation going, and improves your response time.

- Use the interviewer's title (Mr. or Ms. and their last name). Only use the interviewer's first name if they invite you to do so.

- Never interrupt the interviewer. Listen, wait for a pause, and then respond accordingly.

- If there are several interviewers on the phone simultaneously, try to keep track of who is asking the question. When one interviewer asks you a question, clarify who asked the question so you can respond directly to that person and use their name.

- Give short answers. Don't talk endlessly.

- The goal of a telephone interview is to convince the potential employer to schedule a face-to-face meeting. After you thank the interviewer, ask if it would be possible to meet in person. "Thanks for the opportunity to speak with you about my credentials. I would be honored to work at _____. Would it be possible to schedule a face-to-face meeting?"

- Follow up with a written thank you letter (see page 170).

Section 4:
Navigating your Second Year Successfully

Whether you are dealing with your career services office, trying to get involved in extracurricular activities, or are curious about academic offerings, this section will address some of the most common questions that second-year students ask.

Q. How can I use my career services office effectively during my second year?

A. One of the great assets that a career services office can offer a second-year law student is the gift of objectivity. You may be feeling pressure from family and friends to reach goals that may not be in sync with your actual interests, skills and credentials. The place to get a "reality check"—whether you like the feedback or not—is your career services office.

Generally speaking, the mission of most career services offices is to:

- Facilitate job searches by law students through on-campus interviews, job fairs, postings, and other means;

- Cultivate employer relations;

- Counsel students regarding career options;

- Create informative and interesting programming to facilitate students' career development;

- Collect accurate statistics about employment for associations and publications; and

- Create a network of alumni/ae and friends who support the law school and the hiring of law students and graduates.

While the your career services office facilitates employment, the staff professionals are not legal headhunters and do not place students in jobs. They do not receive bonuses or other monetary rewards for placing students in jobs. This is a major misunderstanding that law students have. They view the office as a placement service; whereas, the role of the office is to take constructive steps to assist students in finding jobs both during law school and following graduation.

The role of career services is to provide a metaphorical job-search table laden with opportunities: educational programs, networking events, one-on-one counseling sessions, on-campus interviews, job fairs, and much more. Your job—no pun intended—is to own the responsibility for assessing your interests and skills and then taking the steps to find the employer who most nearly matches your interests.

Is this a great deal of work? Yes. Frustrating? Sometimes. Time-consuming? Definitely. But will your hard work ultimately pay off in a better résumé, a smarter interview style, and a realistic outlook on the job market. You bet. So don't walk by the career services office because you are scared about what you'll hear. Walk in the door, make the appointment, and take the first step in becoming a sophisticated job searcher.

First Steps

- **Make an appointment.** If you have not done so during your first year, make an appointment at the beginning of your second year and introduce yourself to a staff professional in your career services office. Some schools assign students to particular counselors, others do not. If you are assigned a counselor and you would prefer to meet with another staff professional, then do so!

- **Résumé and cover letter review.** Bring a copy of your résumé and a cover letter for the career services professional to review. Also bring a list of questions or concerns to start your job search process. The more the career services office knows about your interests and credentials, the better off you will be.

- **Know the timelines.** Rather than operate in a vacuum about great job opportunities, figure out the deadlines you must adhere to and put yourself on a schedule to accomplish small tasks every week. Your career services office can help keep you on task for finding a job.

- **Develop a productive working relationship.** Don't be a stranger in your career services office. Drop by at least once a week and say "hello." Sometimes there's a great posting or a telephone call from an employer that day and you're at the right place at the right time. Of course, all postings are made public but you're at an advantage if you can develop a productive working relationship with your career services office.

- **Benefit from the objectivity that your career services office offers.** One of the greatest assets that you can realize from your career services professional staff is maintaining an objective understanding of your interests, assets, and deficits. The career services office wants you to find a job that's right for you—there's no agenda. As a law student, it's easy to lose objectivity and lose yourself to the herd mentality of law school. Parents, family, and friends perceive you in an idealized light. This can be wonderful but it can also be a burden. Allow yourself to hear what the career services office staff sees in you that's unique, wonderful, and different from your classmates.

- **Complain civilly.** If you have complaints about your career services office, first try to resolve them amicably within the office. If you are upset about the range of services or lack of attention, then begin with the immediate staff professional in charge, such as the dean of career services. Taking your complaints to the dean of the law school or the student bar association president escalates the issue and creates animosity. Many law students misunderstand the role of career services and it's an easy place to lash out against the frustration of finding a job. Be constructive in your criticism and work with the staff professionals in career services.

Q. My law school offers certificate programs in specialized areas of legal practice. Are these certificates worthwhile? Will a certificate give me an advantage in the employment market after graduation?

A. Many law schools offer certificates in specific practice areas such as health law, labor and employment law, international law, litigation, and elder law. These certificates offer second- and third-year students the opportunity to specialize and graduate with an extra credential.

Should you earn a specialized certificate, in addition to your J.D. degree? It depends on various factors:

- **Enjoyment quotient.** Do you genuinely enjoy a particular practice area? How much do you enjoy a particular practice area based on real-life experience, prior work experience, or other factors? Does your prior work experience complement the certificate you will be receiving?

> Tip: Don't participate in a certificate program simply because a particular practice area is "hot" this year. What's "hot" this year may not be next year.

- **Your comfort with a narrow academic focus.** How comfortable are you narrowing the remainder of your law school class choices to fulfill your certificate requirements? A certificate program narrows your scope of course choices for the remainder of law school.

- **Compatibility with faculty.** Research the faculty who will be instructing the certificate program. Do you like these professors? Do you look forward to learning from them? Working for them? When you commit to a certificate program, you may be restricting yourself to a narrow selection of faculty members.

- **Job placement success rate.** This is the key factor. You're earning a certificate because you think it's going to boost your employment potential. Ask yourself: Will the certificate leverage your J.D. degree and offer you increased employment opportunities? In particular, when investigating whether or not to register for a certificate program, ask the director of the program these questions:

  - What is your job placement rate for the last three years?
  - What types of special services do you provide to assist certificate program students to find jobs during the summer?
  - What types of special services do you provide to assist third-year students to find jobs following graduation?
  - Are there particular job fairs that focus on this practice area?

- As the director of the certificate program, how involved are you in career development issues?

> Tip: Beware of the certificate program director who views his or her role as solely academic and delegates career development issues to the career services office. If the whole point of specializing through a certificate program is to increase your hiring potential, then the faculty ought to be invested in the hiring process.

- Please give me examples of the types of jobs certificate program graduates have found in the last three years.
- Can you give me the names of two current certificate program participants so I can speak to them myself?

Maintain Your Flexibility

If you decide that a certificate program is a good choice for you, then you ought to nonetheless plan carefully for alternatives. Maintain your flexibility regarding employment options since jobs in your chosen field may be highly competitive or difficult to find in your area. For example, you may want to practice health law but if the market is highly competitive in your area, then keep your options open by:

- **Maintaining two résumés.** It's a smart idea to maintain two résumés, one that focuses on your certificate area of specialization and another than it broader and de-emphasizes your certificate program. This way, you can use the specialty résumé for those employers that specialize in your area, and broaden your appeal to more general employers.

- **Broadening your range of possible employers.** Develop a list of employers who are top-tier choices and practice in your area of interest. However, you must also think more broadly about employers who may not be practicing in your area of interest but who do have practice areas that appeal to you. For example, you may want to practice health law (which has a strong corporate and regulatory skills set); however, at the beginning of your career you may begin in a corporate law department and work to specialize from there.

- **Broadening your geographic range.** Try to be flexible about your geographic range, if possible. For example, if you want to practice a certain type of law, understand that certain practice areas may be clustered in different parts of the country. Sports and entertainment law is clustered mainly in Los Angeles and New York City, with pockets throughout the country. However, you are setting yourself up for failure if you want to practice entertainment law only in Charleston, South Carolina. There are surely entertainment law practitioners there, but they are fewer and farther between.

- **Learning to discuss the transferability of your credentials.** If you earn a certificate in a specific area, you always want to be able to discuss your credentials in a broader sense with potential employers. This means understanding the value of your overall skills. There are certain things that all lawyers know how to do and need to perform in their day-to-day work: in-depth research and analysis, clear writing skills, and persuasive advocacy skills. When you are discussing your credentials with an employer, you must always stress that your academic and practical credentials are excellent and transferable.

For example, if you are interviewing with a general practitioner and they are aware that you have a certificate in international law, then you must address this issue directly and put the employer at ease:

"I truly enjoyed the international law certificate program and gained some important skills that are transferable to a general trial practice and that will benefit your firm. For instance, I conducted in-depth legal research on some very intricate treaty terms and participated in an international trial moot court competition. These are skills that I would bring to you and enable me to be productive very quickly."

Q. My law school offers dual degree options—JD/MBA, JD/PhD, JD/MPH. Are two graduate degrees better than one? Will a dual degree increase my marketability to legal employers?

A. The benefits and detriments of a dual degree are similar to those discussed in the section on certificate programs (page 184). Should you earn a second graduate degree while you're in law school? The answer is: It depends on your professional goals. Most law students like the idea of hedging their bets. If one graduate degree is good, then two degrees must be better, right?

Two graduate degrees are not necessarily better than one.

"Students sometimes believe that a graduate degree in addition to a J.D. will, in and of itself, make them more marketable or increase their earnings potential," observes Robert Kaplan, Associate Dean and Director of Externships at William & Mary School of Law.

"That's not necessarily so. Before devoting time and money to earning a second graduate degree, ask yourself, 'Do I have specific career goals for which the additional degree will be helpful?' If you don't have those specific career objectives, think carefully before participating in a dual degree program. And a dual degree does not automatically translate into a higher starting salary than a student could earn with a law degree alone."

There are market niches where dual degrees may be helpful, but it's important to be strategic. For example, if you want to pursue a career in law school administration, it might make sense to earn a graduate degree in higher education administration. Work in non-profit or corporate management may benefit from an MBA. A master's degree in public policy may open doors in lobbying or government relations.

Consider the following factors when weighing and balancing your decision to earn a dual degree:

- **Dual degree program requirements shift your graduation date.** Often with a dual degree program, instead of graduating in June you need an extra semester to complete your credits and will receive your degree the following December. The June-December shift can be the source of confusion for some legal employers, who may be accustomed to coming on campus to interview, making offers, and starting a new associate class at a specific time (often in the early fall). As a dual degree student with a delayed graduation date, do you qualify for on-campus interviews as a second-year student for two summers or one? How will law firms characterize your status—are you a third-year or a second-year for the purposes of the summer?

- **Dual degree students need to think through the timing im-**

plications for their job search.
Depending on your non-law class
schedule and other graduate
school requirements, you may find
it difficult to participate in your
law school's on-campus interviews
or off-campus interview programs.
Scheduling and sequencing of non-
law classes and non-law internship
requirements may interfere with
your ability to complete summer
legal internships after your first or
second year.

· **Legal employers may view you
with suspicion.** Get ready to go on
the defensive and explain why you
want to be a lawyer. As a dual degree student, you may find that law
firms will question your dedication
to becoming a lawyer. "Some legal
employers may question whether
a dual degree student is fully committed to practicing law," says
Robert Kaplan of William & Mary.
"Law firms may think that the student earned an additional degree
to pave the way for a non-law career down the road and therefore
may be reluctant to invest in the
student. Be prepared, therefore,
to provide very specific reasons in
interviews for how the additional
degree will be meaningful for the
traditional practice of law. Non-
legal employers may have similar
concerns. 'If this student wants to
be a hospital administrator,' they

may wonder, 'why did she invest the time, energy and money in a law degree? Does she ultimately want to practice law instead of being a health care professional?'"

Before you register for a dual degree program and commit your time and money, ask yourself the following questions:

- **How marketable is a dual degree with my professional goals?** If you are going to law school to practice law, then earn your J.D. degree and practice law. Remember, earning multiple graduate degrees does not guarantee anything (aside from tremendous student loan payments and much explaining to potential employers).

- **Whose life is it anyway?** If you are earning a dual degree as a means to an end, then think carefully about what you want to achieve. If you are in law school because your parents want to tell their friends that you're a lawyer but you really want to run your own retail business, then consider whose life you are living. If your father is focused on you becoming a lawyer, consider sending him an application and suggest that he earn the J.D. degree, not you.

- **What kind of career services assistance can I expect?** Does your school's career services office have experience handling dual degree students? Will they be able to advise you and guide you to employers who will appreciate your credentials? Are there graduates who have trodden this path and would they be willing to mentor you?

- **What is the reputation of the graduate degree program?** The caliber of a university's professional and graduate degree programs sometimes varies greatly. If, for example, the reputation of a non-law graduate program lags significantly behind the law school's reputation, you may want to factor that into the equation. Even if your grades in the non-law program are stronger than your law school grades, you'll want to consider whether any disparity in reputation between the programs outweighs the potential benefits of the higher GPA and the additional degree.

- **Will the faculty take an active role in my employment?** Do the faculty members involved in the dual degree curriculum communicate and understand the goals of the program? Are they working in tandem to make this an efficient use of your time and money?

Alternatives to Dual Degree Programs

There are alternatives to committing time and money to a dual degree program. Consider taking courses in another graduate school program short of earning a degree. That will enable you to gain exposure to a different discipline, network and develop contacts, and gain an understanding of a field that complements your legal studies. You also may want to work for academic credit in a non-law externship. Your law school career services office likely will have non-law contacts and be able to refer you to alumni in your field of interest with whom you can extern. Career services offices in other departments of the university also may provide externship referrals.

Bottom line: Dual degree programs can be wonderful for some students, but they can present employment challenges. Don't be fooled into believing there's a magical configuration of graduate degrees out there. If you want to be a lawyer, earn your J.D. degree. If you don't want to be a lawyer, then conduct the research and find the right graduate degree for you.

Q. My law school offers several clinics. I need to decide whether or not to register for a clinic program for my third year. Are clinics worthwhile? How can I leverage clinic experience in my job search?

A. Clinics offers second-year law students the opportunity to experience the practice of law under the guidance of a supervisor who is both a teacher and practitioner. "Clinics offer students a sense of what it means to lawyer," observes Martha Rayner, Associate Clinical Professor of Law at Fordham University School of Law. "Some students come to law school and they don't really know what a lawyer does and many don't know what type of law they want to practice. Clinic is an opportunity to experiment, step into the shoes of a lawyer, and see if you enjoy the work. Through experience, you can decide if you more interested in trial practice, appellate law, policy or something else."

Rayner, who teaches at Fordham's International Justice Clinic, notes " Clinics are also an incredible learning opportunity to actually do research that's connected to a client, write papers, draft e-mails and letters, and conduct investigations. Because clinics are also academic opportunities, time is set aside to reflect on what you did, what worked, what didn't work, and to apply that new knowledge in practice someday."

Clinical experience translates into:
- Experience to build your résumé

- An opportunity to test-drive a practice area decide what you truly enjoy

- Lawyering skills that can be transferred to any lawyering context

- A mentoring relationship with a professor

- Networking opportunities

Bottom line: Any clinic experience is valuable. Find a subject matter that appeals to you, but—most importantly - get out there and do the work. The theory and skills you learn will be transferable to many other lawyering contexts.

American Inns of Court

Does your school offer an American Inns of Court? According to its web site (www.innsofcourt.org), the American Inns of Court "are designed to improve the skills, professionalism and ethics of the bench and bar." Many law schools now have American Inns of Court "pupillage teams" consisting of law students, law firm associates, partners and judges. Each Inn meets approximately once a month to hold programs and discuss issues related to ethics, skills, and professionalism. Some Inns specialize in particular areas of practice, but most are general in scope. Law students have an opportunity to study with seasoned professionals, develop mentor relationships, and learn more about the profession. If your law school offers an American Inns of Court opportunity, consider taking advantage of this very special chance to learn and grow as a professional.

Q. Should I join a study group?

A. It depends. For some students, a study group is both a peer support system and an academic lifeboat. For others, a study group drains time away from solitary study and research. In truth, the answer probably lies somewhere in between.

If you are a student who thrives on social interactions and enjoys the give-and-take of a study group environment, then go forth and organize one. Keep in mind that your study group should be composed of smart, committed, and academically savvy individuals. If you feel like you're the smartest member of your study group, then you may not be getting the full advantage of your bargain.

Avoid forming a study group early in the semester. Get to know your fellow classmates before making a commitment. Listen to how your classmates answer questions in class. Identify individuals who are prepared and committed to academic success. Some students enjoy solitary study during the semester. As exam time approaches, however, you may find that a study group will help you stay focused, solve problems, and learn from others. In other words, stop, look and listen before organizing or joining a study group. Otherwise you may find yourself saddled with more problems than you started with.

Getting Started

· To organize a study group, begin by asking two or three classmates to join you. There's no ideal size for a study group, but five is probably the maximum number of people.

- Seek out a diverse group of classmates in order to hear and understand the many facets of an issue.

- Set a meeting date and time that works for everyone. Scheduling regular meetings helps keep the momentum.

- Find a meeting location that has few distractions and allows you to engage in spirited conversations. Most law libraries have study rooms that you can reserve. Nearby public libraries offer an off-site option for those who need to separate from the law school environment. Some students enjoy meeting in other people's apartments or at a local café. Choose a place that's convenient and conducive to group study.

- Create the parameters so everyone understands what is expected. Will the study group meet to discuss all courses or just a select few? Will the group meet daily, weekly, biweekly, monthly? How many hours will you meet?

Bottom line: Whether or not you choose to join a study group is up to you. Some students thrive in group study environments; others perform better when they study alone. If you do decide that a study group is a good route for you, seek out diverse individuals whom you respect and who are similarly committed to academic success.

Q. I have a learning disability. What can I do to improve my chances of academic success?

A. The Americans with Disabilities Act (ADA) states that a disability means, with respect to an individual: 1) a physical or mental impairment that substantially limits one or more major life activities; and 2) a record of such impairment; or 3) being regarded as having such impairment.

The most common disorders presented by law students requesting accommodations are Attention Deficit Disorder (ADD) or Attention Deficit Hyperactivity Disorder (ADHD), which may fall under the ADA definition of a disability.

If you have a disability, you are not alone. According to the Law School Admission Council (LSAC), in 2006 there were 1,922 requests for accommodations by students who took the LSAT. In an ABA report entitled "Goal IX: A Report on the Status of the Participation of Persons with Disabilities in ABA Leadership," 2,180 lawyers who responded to a professional census survey indicated that they had disabilities. The ABA report also stated that in 2005, law schools provided accommodations for 3,400 law students throughout the U.S.

LaRasz Moody, Director of Academic Support at Villanova University School of Law, offers the following advice for law students:

1. If you require accommodations in the classroom or for exams, inform the school that you have a disability or impairment.

2. You must ask for accommodations and do so early, well in advance of final exams.

3. If you believe that you may have a learning disability, you are responsible for providing a current diagnostic psychoeducational evaluation to the school.

4. Ask if the law school has a disability coordinator and work with that person to get information on what the school requires for accommodation requests.

Does your law school have an Office of Academic Support? Ask.

According to Ms. Moody, a lawyer and a former social worker, "It's important to get as comprehensive a diagnostic report as possible, preferably from a testing psychologist. Reports from medical doctors are not usually acceptable; it's best to obtain an evaluation from a testing psychologist to support your request for accommodation."

"There's no downside to identifying yourself as a student with a disability," notes Ms. Moody. "Some students fear that a learning disability is a stigma. This could not be further from the truth. If a student needs an accommodation to be on a level education ground as other students, they would be doing themselves a disservice by not requesting an accommodation."

Looking ahead to graduation and the bar exam, students with disabilities who require accommodations need to research the specific bar examiner web site for state-specific information about accommodations for the bar exam. You will need to know:

- What documentation is required in your specific jurisdiction in order to establish a disability and receive accommodation; and

- What the time line is for submitting your accommodation requests.

Accommodations in law school are no guarantee that accommodations will be offered to you for the bar exam.

For more information:

www.ahead.org—AHEAD is a professional association committed to full participation of persons with disabilities in postsecondary education. Their web site contains many excellent resources for students and educators.

www.add.org—Since 1989, the Attention Deficit Disorder Association (ADDA) has provided information, resources and networking to adults with AD/HD and to the professionals who work with them.

http://www.abanet.org/disability/docs/conf_report_final.pdf—Report and Recommendation from the 2006 National Conference on the Employment of Lawyers with Disabilities. Also see www.abanet.org/disability for the ABA Commission on Mental and Physical Disability Law.

http://www.eeoc.gov/facts/accommodations-attorneys.html—"Reasonable Accommodations for Attorneys with Disabilities."

Find a Mentor!

The American Bar Association's Commission on Mental and Physical Disability Law established a Mentor Program for law students with disabilities, prospective law students with disabilities, and recent law school graduates with disabilities to give members of these groups the opportunity to learn from an experienced attorney. Check out their web site at http://www.abanet.org/disability/subcommittee/mentor.shtml.

Students can complete a mentee form online. Based on your answers, you will be matched with a mentee. At that point, how the mentoring relationship progresses is up to the individuals. According to Jonathan Simeone of the American Bar Association, over the past five years, approximately 100 mentor-mentee matches have been made.

Q. Between law school and college loans, I'm looking at a huge amount of post-graduate debt. How do I project the amount of money I will owe after I graduate from law school? What steps can I take to minimize my student loans?

A. Student loan debt can impact your career choices.

The following are some suggestions to help you minimize and manage your student loan debt, and plan effectively so that you have the most freedom to choose the career path that works for you:

- Know your exact student loan debt amount and when your payment obligations begin. This is very important information going forward. To figure out your amount and payment schedule, visit your law school financial aid office. Talk to the staff professional in charge and understand your obligations.

- Once you understand your monthly loan repayment obligations, it will help you create a budget and required salary. Thus, when an employer asks "what are your salary requirements?," you can answer with a realistic number based on facts.

- Learn about reputable loan consolidation options. If you have both college and law school loans, then it's a good idea to figure out consolidation options. This might enable you to take a lower paying job while still repaying your loan obligation.

- Live frugally while in law school. While it's tempting to splurge, stay within a strict budget while in law school. Avoid incurring any credit card debt to live above your means. Lifestyle borrowing sets the stage for poor money management habits in the future. An excellent book to consult is *Your Money or Your Life* by Joe Dominguez and Vicki Robin (Penguin, 1999).

- Work part-time, if possible, during your second and third years of law school. Not only do you gain valuable experience, but you can save money that will enable you to make better career choices in the future.

Congratulations!

You have successfully navigated your second year of law school. Most lawyers agree that the second year is the most stressful in terms of balancing academic and career demands. Have a wonderful summer and get ready for your third and final year.

Preparing for Your Third Year

What's next? Savvy students plan ahead and anticipate what will happen during their third year of law school as you inch toward graduation.

Volume Three of *Asked and Answered* features practical advice to make your third year of law school your most successful year.

- Bar exam issues—tips to succeed
- Job hunting tips—strategies for finding a full-time job
  - Cover letters
  - Résumés
  - Interview tips
- Financial aid and student loan repayment
- Alumni associations and bar associations
- Graduation tips
- LL.M. programs—in your future?
- Non-traditional career tips